"Bill Eshelman has written a wonderful account of his reflections while serving his year in Vietnam. Through the letters to his wife, Pat, at the time he served there as a young officer, he has recaptured the thoughts, impressions, and feelings of a Marine at war in a strange environment. Those of us who share his experiences can easily relate to his story. This is a great read for all who want to experience Vietnam first hand as it was experienced by a young Marine at the time."

–GENERAL ANTHONY C. ZINNI, USMC (RETIRED)

"First and foremost, the book is extremely well written and meaningful. Publishing the book can do a significant service to all Marines who served in Vietnam, particularly those who served as covans to the VNMC. The frustrations and personal internal conflicts described are shared by many, if not all of us. They certainly strike a chord with me.

"There have been many accounts of this conflict, but most have been focused at the national, Vietnam theater or combat unit level. Eshelman brings the conflict to the level of the individual young Marine Officer, trying to do the job his country has sent him to do, with all the real emotions and questions that ran through our minds. In sharing his detailed thoughts, through frequent letters to Pat, he will open that world to many who could not enter it otherwise. I applaud the dedication and talent in writing this wonderful book."

–LIEUTENANT GENERAL JAMES A. BRABHAM, JR., USMC (RETIRED)

"Once I got started, I had a hard time stopping—awaiting the next day or two—to see what happened. I like the format and the mixing of planning, combat, experiences with higher headquarters, side comments on the war in general, some appropriate pictures, and personal feelings at different times of the character and fighting ability of the individual Viet Nam Marines.

"I personally think the book is an easy read and was made better by the added explanation in italics. The coverage of the Tet Offensive is compelling."

-COLONEL JOSEPH FLYNN, USMC (RETIRED)

"I have now finished reading *Letters to Pat*—wishing there was even more yet! It should be a best seller—but more important, it should be required reading for those aspiring to be Marine officers.

"Eshelman shows an intimate recollection of immersion with a TQLC infantry battalion in combat, sharing the extreme hardships, and skillfully advising/supporting a reluctant counterpart battalion commander . . . with the patience of Job!

"He has created a most credible and unique insider, on the ground, vivid account (in constant rain, extreme heat, streams, mud/muck and otherwise jungle conditions) of what it was like in 1967-68 in RVN, including the Tet offensive and Hue City/Citadel siege—now 50 years ago."

-COLONEL JAMES H. TINSLEY, USMC (RETIRED)

"I completely concur with Eshelman's conclusions. Despite his valor, we as a Country didn't appreciate the staying power and history of NVN. They won and we lost.

"I really enjoyed this superbly written book, the feelings, the dedication and the honesty. The self-effacing style and clear courage shown are why I am such a fan of our Marine Corps."

-CAPTAIN ROBIN BATTAGLINI, USN (RETIRED)

"A really good read. I particularly enjoyed the discussion of the '68 Tet fight in Saigon and Hue Citadel. The assessment of the VNMC performance mirrors mine in 1970-71. I wish this book had been available for me to read before my tour as an advisor. The insights on counterpart relationship and frustration with trying to improve VNMC operational effectiveness would have helped me do a better job."

-COLONEL JAMES McCLUNG, USMC (RETIRED)

"Providing military advisors to foreign security forces continues to be a key component of US National Security Strategy. Eshelman's *"Letters to Pat,"* drawn from his letters and journal written during his service in Vietnam, will be of value to anyone with either a historical interest or an interest in advisory efforts today. Counterpart relationships, cultural differences, support from higher authority, and physical hardships are among the relevant aspects covered in a clear and direct writing style."

-COLONEL WILLIAM FITE, USMC (RETIRED)

"Eshelman is a very talented writer. After reading the book I know exactly what he did and how he tried to make the ARVN chain of command work instead of over reliance on using the advisor channels. Knowing many of those he served with made the book even more interesting to me. The strength of our Corps is the advantage we have knowing each other.

"That said, I think all Covans would be interested in this book, as well as anyone else interested in the Vietnam War. I would recommend it to any university with a military history department, including West Point and Annapolis."

-LIEUTENANT COLONEL E. GEORGE RIVERS, USMC (RETIRED)

"I found Eshelman's recounting of the daily life of a Marine, especially as an advisor to the Vietnamese military, compelling. The book brings vividly to life struggles experienced in trying to coordinate US and South Vietnamese military activities. At times he sees the US attitude toward the South Vietnamese as the problem; at other times he reflects on the failure of the Vietnamese to assume responsibility for what should have been properly theirs. The Vietnamese 'have learned that if they drag their feet long enough, the advisor will use US assets to accomplish the mission while they watch.'

The work also describes the failure to successfully pacify hamlets, coping with sickness and battlefield wounds (his own and others), grieving the death of companions, enduring the rain, missing his family, the constant demand for numbers that were in the process of being passed on often inflated, and emerging questions about the way the whole conflict was being prosecuted, and the emerging sense of the 'senseless nature of it all.'

"In addition, Eshelman recounts memorably what it means to go for extended periods without toilets, hot water, clean body and clothes while at the same time daily wading through muddy water up to one's shoulders, while engaging an enemy that appears and then quickly vanishes. Yet the letters also reflect the ongoing desire of one trained to fight, to actually engage in combat, to be tested on the battlefield, to 'miss not being in the action', a desire most civilians, I am confident, have never come close to experiencing.

"Living with death and the reality of the matter-of-fact documenting and reporting of death and often the lack of time to be emotional about it all at the time is a matter Eshelman also reflects on as he looks back on his experiences.

"I also found commendable his effort to engage with the Vietnamese by learning their language, eating their food, and, in general, socializing with them.

"Finally, Eshelman gets off his chest his often-experienced feeling that "the only people who want[ed] the war to end [were] the peasants. The Vietnamese politicians and the upper ranking military officers . . . never had it better . . . what with payoffs from a thriving black market."

"Among the many striking statements in the book is the one to be taken in the context of doing what one has been trained to do and asked by your country to do: "It does no good to attempt to weigh the good and the bad. There is no good, and I reject the bad in order to live with myself."

–Dr. Robert M. Baird, Emeritus Professor of Philosophy, Baylor University

Letters to Pat: A Year in the Life of a Vietnam Marine
by Bill Eshelman, USMC retired

ISBN 978-1-63393-860-1

Published by

 köehlerbooks™

210 60th Street
Virginia Beach, VA 23451
800–435–4811
www.koehlerbooks.com

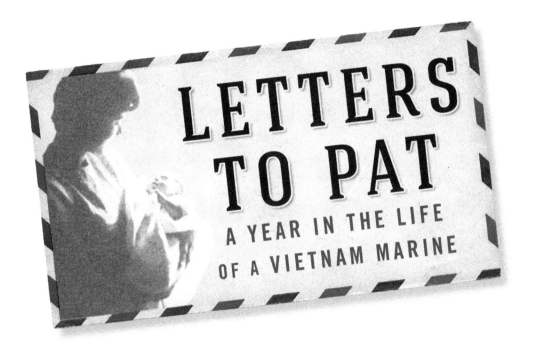

BILL ESHELMAN
USMC RETIRED

VIRGINIA BEACH
CAPE CHARLES

Dedicated to those fallen Marines whom I had taught and with whom I later served; and to my wife Pat, now deceased, who in many ways had a tougher time than I did, as she lived through the war by reading my many letters which follow in paraphrased form.

TABLE OF CONTENTS

PAT HOLDING BABY CATHY 1967 COLORADO AVE

PAT WITH FAMILY 1967 COLORADO AVE

PAT AND I 1968 R&R HONOLULU.

PAT R&R IN HONOLULU, 1968

PROLOGUE

IN HOPES OF putting that year in better perspective and perhaps to help understand some of my motivations at the time, I offer the following earlier events in my life:

Fifty-eight of us, who graduated from the US Naval Academy (USNA) with the class of 1959, volunteered and were selected to be commissioned as second lieutenants (2nd Lts.) in the US Marine Corps headed for The Basic School (TBS) at Quantico, Virginia. There we would be transformed into Marine lieutenants capable of leading other young Marines. The ethos of "every Marine a rifleman first" was embedded in us from the beginning. Before graduating from the academy, however, several of us had requested and qualified for aviation options, meaning we would be ordered to flight school at the Naval Air Station, Pensacola, Florida, after completing TBS.

My primary interest in becoming a Marine, and more specifically a Marine pilot, was a result of our midshipman cruise the summer before our senior year. I was assigned to the USS Saratoga, a large aircraft carrier in the Mediterranean at the time, which had a Marine aircraft squadron aboard. In mid-July 1958, the pro-Western monarch of Lebanon was murdered, and our ship was ordered to respond. We left Marines and sailors on the beach in Cannes, France as our ship departed during the night! I was impressed with the young Marine pilots flying missions and enjoyed many hours in their ready room talking with them. By the end of the summer, I was convinced that this was what I wanted to do! Later, though, before our eight months at Quantico were completed, I had begun to have second thoughts about aviation. I was starting to enjoy being in the field, the weapons training, and the opportunity to lead Marines on the ground. I wondered if I would ever regret not leading an infantry platoon of young Marines. Nevertheless, I continued to follow my original decision and soon found myself in Pensacola, Florida.

By the time I had completed pre-flight and soloed the T-34 aircraft, I had begun to think seriously about dropping out of flight school for other reasons. I had become very involved with one of the churches in Pensacola and was teaching a junior high school Sunday school class, as well as working with the youth on Wednesday evenings. As a result, the pastor had encouraged me to consider going to seminary and becoming a pastor after I'd completed my military obligation. He and I traveled to Atlanta one weekend and met a professor he knew at Emory University, who also encouraged me to consider the ministry.

At this point, I knew that if I completed flight training, I would be committed to remaining in the service an extra year or more before I could begin studies at Emory. And so, after some deep soul-searching, I requested to be dropped from the flight program and ordered to a Marine division, where I might serve for the rest of my four-year commitment. But before I did, the senior officer who interviewed me made sure I understood that this would be a career killer! That was okay with me at the time since I was planning on leaving the Marine Corps after four years anyway. I could not have imagined back then how future events would reshape my life.

Much to my satisfaction, I was assigned to the 2nd Marine Division at Camp LeJeune, North Carolina, doing all the things I had learned at TBS. It wasn't long before I knew I had made the right decision, but maybe not for the right reason. Time would tell.

After Camp LeJeune, which included deployments to Guantanamo Bay, Cuba during both the Bay of Pigs disaster and the successful Cuban missile crisis, I completed my four-year service commitment in Japan. On my return to the US, I was given an opportunity to go back to TBS as an instructor and jumped at the chance. To my way of thinking, there were some improvements needed in the instruction there, and I wanted to be part of it. Additionally, Pat and I were now married with two wonderful children: a third would follow, and this assignment would allow me some quality time with my family.

But about the same time, Southeast Asia had begun to rumble. Not long afterward, the lieutenants that we were instructing at TBS were being sent straight to Vietnam. Before my turn would come, since I had recently returned from a year in Japan, Pat and I would find ourselves at Arlington National Cemetery standing next to the widows of those I had taught not so long ago. Although I'd completed my USNA obligation, how could I not follow these lieutenants?

As my letters begin, you may sense my overwhelming desire and urgency to serve as an infantry company commander in Vietnam. I had been part of a small group of Marine officer instructors at TBS, highly trained in the art and execution of small-unit tactics, and had taught the lieutenants who were now being combat-tested. We, however, had not been. We all felt the need to be tested . . . and we all knew the ultimate test for a Marine infantry captain was to serve as a company commander in combat. Pat, a Marine wife for the last seven years, understood this.

We also knew that the Vietnam War had accelerated promotions, and that would limit my remaining time as a captain. Therefore, as a backup plan, several of us requested and went through the MATA (Military Assistance Training for Advisors) school at Ft. Bragg, North Carolina, before leaving for Vietnam. In our view, since most majors in Marine units were becoming staff officers, being an advisor with the Vietnamese would provide a first-hand look at the war even if we were not able to command a company before being promoted. Little did I know how fast promotions would happen. Nevertheless, as I arrived in Vietnam grasping for straws, I thought maybe I still had a chance to command an infantry company in combat. It was worth a try!

As I share the events that I described almost daily to Pat in each of my letters, I will try to retain the exact wording in them while leaving out the personal family dialogue that obviously was also heavy on my mind. Occasionally, I will expand on the original text using italics to add notes from my combat journal, as well as referring to later events that might help the reader better understand the current situation. My overall intent is to share my thoughts on Vietnam and the war as I lived it day by day.

Lastly, please keep in mind that the age of the computer and iPhone with its texting and email capabilities had not yet arrived, so it took days and weeks to correspond between Vietnam and the US. There were times when Pat could follow my whereabouts in Vietnam much faster by reading the Washington Post than waiting for my next letter to arrive.

1

15 OCT 67—*written from the 7th Marines Regimental CP (Command Post) outside of Đà nẵng*

After flying cross-country from Washington, DC, the wait in San Francisco to continue my journey to Vietnam seemed to be forever, especially after finding out that the promotion list to Major had been published. I sat and mulled that over for several hours, and then discovered that I had been taken off the manifest for my flight to Okinawa, the staging area for entry into Vietnam.

I floundered around for a while in the terminal, but finally found a young corporal who agreed to add me back to the manifest. It turned out to be a commercially chartered "Continental with the Golden Tail." That was a good thing, but bad luck was not far away.

The flight was delayed twice, but we finally got airborne about 11 am. I had made friends earlier with a Gunnery Sergeant but was split up from the "Gunny" when we went on board due to the military precedence of loading . . . dependents, officers, and then enlisted. So I joined forces with an LDO (Limited Duty Officer), and we sat in a middle row, where the stewardess decided that directly across from us would be the perfect spot for a momma and her three kids: one baby and two boys, almost identical to Charlie's boys.

Charlie Davis, his wife Claire, and Pat and I had met each other at Camp LeJeune, NC while Charlie and I were Lts assigned to the Aerial Observation School (a follow-on assignment after serving as a platoon commander). AO school emphasized identifying targets; calling for artillery, air, and naval gunfire support; and adjusting the rounds or bombs onto the target. This knowledge would prove invaluable to both of us during our time in Vietnam.

After Camp LeJeune, I was sent to Japan for a year, and Charlie served aboard a US Navy cruiser. A few years later we found ourselves as neighbors in Woodbridge, Virginia, teaching at TBS. More importantly, we have remained good friends over the years. As I headed toward Vietnam, Charlie was serving with the 1st Battalion, 26th Marine Regiment located along the Vietnamese DMZ (demilitarized zone). He had been a company commander and was now a battalion operations officer.

The seating arrangement on the Continental turned out to be a good thing since the mother didn't use her fourth seat, giving the LDO and me the only extra seat on the entire plane! It proved invaluable on the leg from Honolulu to Okinawa, which took another five hours, after we had suffered a three-hour time loss before landing at Hickam Air Force Base (AFB), Honolulu.

The Continental was much nicer than the military transport that flew me overseas in 1963. The hot meals were excellent, and the service was outstanding. When we landed at Kadena AFB, Okinawa, it was raining, and I got soaked. We were taken to Camp Hansen and checked in for an approximate 48-hour layover. It was now Monday night at about 8 pm. We had crossed the International Date Line, picked up a day, but lost three more hours.

1st Lt Norton checked us in. He remembered me teaching tactics at TBS, which would prove helpful later. After being wounded three times in Vietnam and awarded three Purple Hearts, he had been evacuated to Okinawa to complete his one-year tour. I arrived at the BOQ (bachelor officers' quarters) and was assigned a two-man room with shared bathroom, finally got some sleep, and woke up the next morning refreshed. My roommate was fresh out of TBS, a "gung-ho" 03 (infantry designation) Lieutenant. He turned out to be a Walter Johnson graduate (*a high school in Silver Spring, Maryland, close to where Pat and I had attended*). He was accommodating. Tuesday, I went to sickbay and received the last of all the shots required before entering Vietnam, picked up some things at the PX (Post Exchange), and found out at 3 pm that I was leaving that evening . . . less than 24 hours after we had landed.

Just before time to muster for the flight, Lt Norton called to say that a modification to my orders had arrived, dated 6 October. I was to report by 9 December as an Advisor to the VNMC (Vietnamese Marine Corps) as part of MACV (Military Assistance Command, Vietnam). Hurray for Tom Hemmingway, my monitor (the infantry assignment officer for the Marine Corps in Washington), who had sent me to the MATA school. Lt Norton also said that because of my new orders, they would have to bump me off of the flight to Đà nẵng and put me on one to Sài gòn, where MACV Hq was located. But after we talked for a while, he put the orders in a lower desk drawer, closed it, and retired for the rest of the day. He told me that when he finds them the next morning, I'll already be in Đà nẵng!

While in Okinawa I ran into several other people that I knew, from lieutenants to majors. I found out that the 5th Marine Regiment might offer the best opportunity to command an infantry company since Phil Shaw and a couple of others that I knew at TBS were in the battalions of that regiment. *Phil and his wife were also Woodbridge neighbors.*

I did make it to Đà nẵng, finally arriving at midnight. It was raining there, too. I had my first "combat command." Being the senior Marine aboard the plane, I was assigned as the Officer in Charge . . . The weight of being a selected major was almost too much for me! Ha! Ha!

Approaching Đà nẵng, we were greeted by flares and several volleys of naval gunfire along the shoreline, which made it quite interesting looking out the window and not knowing what was happening! After landing in the middle of the night, in the rain, in the dark (no lights due to enemy fire), the five officers with me and I stumbled into a little 14-bunk hut where we spent the night. It turned out to be right next to the end of the runway. It took a while to get used to the transports coming in and out, but then the jet fighters started taking off . . . and I thought the first one was coming right through our hut! I think I rose up about 18 inches off my bunk along with everyone else! And that ended any chance of sleep for the night.

I finally found my way to the 1st Division Hq (headquarters) on Wednesday morning, only to find out that all "major" selectees were being assigned as majors, not captains, taking away any chance for me to be assigned to an infantry company. I pleaded with the division personnel officer and told him of my upcoming MACV assignment, and he agreed to talk with the Commanding General. It must have worked because the next morning, I was sent to the 7th Marine Regiment. Bill U'ren (from TBS) was there, and LtCol (Lieutenant Colonel) Barnard (served with him at Camp LeJeune) was the commanding officer of the 3rd Battalion. I will try to be reassigned there. My time is limited, but if I don't get a company, it will not be because I didn't try!

20 OCT 67—*written from the 3rd Battalion, 7th Marines (3/7) outside Đà nẵng*

Much has happened during the last few days . . . I discovered the war but have not yet become part of it. Needless to say, I am disappointed in that particular respect. Let me backtrack.

Two days ago, I caught a ride to the 7th Marines regimental headquarters. The truck ride was uneventful, although the countryside was far from being pacified. Their CP (command post) is located at the top of a hill southwest of Đà nẵng and overlooks the entire area. At Regiment I found the Logistics Officer to be Merrill Sweitzer (from TBS) and was immediately fixed up with a place to sleep. I also ran into more Lts who remembered me from TBS. Later I saw Maj (Major) Woeckner, whom I knew pretty well at TBS. He was getting ready to take over as the Executive Officer of the 3rd Battalion with LtCol Barnard commanding! After I gave another sob story to the Personnel Officer and the Colonel commanding the 7th Marines, I was assigned to 3rd Battalion. However, I didn't find out about the assignment until the next morning. While waiting the day before, I went down to K Company where Hank Thomas (from TBS) had a company and watched firefights with him until about 2 am. The Viet Cong (VC) and

Marines made continuous contacts all around the hill. The day was full of air strikes in every direction. But once again, watching from the hill was almost like being in the states. I said almost!

I had high hopes of getting K Co since Hank was moving up to replace the Battalion Operations Officer, Maj Poland, who was rotating back to the states.

Maj Poland had been one of my previous monitors, who surprised me in 1963 with a set of orders to Iwakuni, Japan, unaccompanied for a year! This, after telling me earlier that I was going to Evanston, Illinois, with my family for two years.

The next morning, I rode out to the 3/7 CP with Maj Woeckner. There, at a beautiful old French Fort was where the 3/7 staff resided. Once again, there were no incidents on the road, but this time I carried a loaded M-16 rifle! Oh yes, I saw Joe Adams (from TBS) on the hill. He was the Operations Officer of the artillery battalion supporting the 7th Marines. I also saw Cleat Oakley (from TBS) at Division Hq in Đà nẵng. He had just talked with Doug Ammon (from TBS) this past weekend. It seems like all of us who served together at Quantico last year have been sent to Vietnam, and many of us are now in the 1st Marine Division.

The weather here requires a cover at night, but during the day it is warm. They serve ice cream in the mess hall! All the huts have electricity. The only real discomfort so far is the cold water for showers and shaving.

There soon would come a time when I would be happy to have any running water!

Here at the Fort, there are more lieutenants who remember me and I them. LtCol Barnard also remembered me. We had a very long talk ranging back to our days in the 2nd Battalion, 2nd Marines and everything in between. He too sympathized with my plight and promised to try to send me to a company. Meanwhile, he wanted me to work as the Assistant Operations Officer and visit all the companies to get snapped into the routine.

Two hours later, they called down and said they had changed their mind and were transferring me to the 2nd Battalion, 7th Marines tomorrow! There would be two companies opening up there. Maj Wayne Swenson (*from TBS and Woodbridge neighborhood*) is the Operations Officer. They are scheduled for a good-sized operation coming up soon. Perhaps my luck is still holding, but time is running out for me to command a company . . . about five more weeks.

2

I finally made it to a Marine battalion with a real job! Albeit not the one I wanted. I left the 3rd Battalion yesterday and drove back in a Jeep to the 7th Marines at 60 mph with my loaded M-16 rifle. They call it "Liberty Road" because the VC ambush us whenever they feel like it!

About noon, Wayne and LtCol Love picked me up at the 7th Marines CP, and I rode back to the 2nd Battalion with them. LtCol Love is the Battalion Commander and seemed to be very understanding of my situation. But since he had already promised his next available company to his Logistics Officer, Captain Mac McIver, it looks like I will end up being a logistician for now and have to wait my turn for another company to open up.

Years later, as a lieutenant colonel, Mac would bring back the 1st Battalion, 4th Marines from Okinawa to 29 Palms, California, and I would take command of the battalion there in 1979 at the Marine Air Ground Training Center.

I like the new job but hope it is for a short time! The battalion is preparing to go on an operation which will last about two weeks, but as the Logistics Officer, I will be in the rear with the gear, doggone it!

On a different note, there is financial hope for a new pay bill to be passed retroactively to the first of October. My pay raise as a major will be about $75/month, and if I put that monthly raise in the bank until I leave Vietnam, the government will add 10% interest. Maybe we can finally save something.

1 NOV 67

Operation Knox is over. We didn't have much excitement, but I thoroughly enjoyed seeing the people and countryside. I was surprised at how easy it was to adjust to my new situation . . . It must have been that good old Marine training! During the past week I climbed mountains that went up into the clouds, walked through rice paddies up to my knees, blasted landing zones out of the jungle for helicopter resupply, bathed in streams, was sunburned by day and frozen by night, had to hunt water to drink, and enjoyed every minute of it! Because of the water shortage, I went three days before I could shave. I was pretty scruffy.

It is at once evident that there is a war going on. I can see it in the faces of the people. I can see it in the bomb craters, the destroyed buildings, bridges, and roads. I hear it in the constant firing of big guns, little guns, air strikes, hand grenades, and other explosions. I'm adjusting, though, because I hardly notice anymore . . . unless it is close! I am finally starting to sleep through most nights.

It was reminiscent of what I had seen in the faces of the older Japanese when I had visited Hiroshima during my 1963-64 tour in Japan . . . and what I remembered from the faces of the older Germans in Hamburg when I had visited as a young USNA Midshipman on a summer cruise in 1956.

My modification of orders to the 2nd Battalion arrived while we were on the operation, but I am still expected to be in Sài gòn by 9 December. The Battalion Executive Officer recommended that I go straight to a company, but I was pretty sure LtCol Love would keep me as the Logistics Officer until the next company was available before making any decision. I was right!

2 NOV 67

Last night, I stayed up late working on an after-action report. Today I had the watch in the Combat Operations Center (COC) where all the radios are located (so that we can monitor and react if necessary to activity in any of our units).

This morning, for a couple of joyful hours, I came as close as I ever will to having a rifle company in combat. I made one last attempt to convince the colonel, and he almost bought it. In fact, he called in the Lt in command of the company (another one of my TBS students) and left it up to him. After a long discussion, it was finally decided that the time was just too short. I will be the Logistics Officer until detached. I feel now that I have made every effort possible to have a combat command.

In all honesty, it would not have been fair to the other Marines in the company for me to have taken over just for a few weeks and then left. It would have been selfish on my part.

Here are a few more details to better outline the war as I am seeing it right now. On Operation Knox, we lifted out by helo (helicopter) one morning and attempted to surprise a VC unit operating in the mountains close by Dong Top, just northeast of Đà nẵng and south of Highway #1, where it runs east-west. We took no fire going in and made no contact the first day, although we were starting to find numerous bunkers and fighting holes. Moving up quickly to the high ground, we suffered quite a few heat casualties, which were subsequently evacuated. As we climbed higher, the tree canopy also became higher, until finally, it was impossible to land helos without clearing an LZ (landing zone) with explosives. This we did several times in order to receive supplies. The helos flew down low and pushed out the supplies from about 20 feet up.

Water was a problem, partially solved by several streams sparsely located and widely separated. This situation led to an unfortunate incident the second night when one of our Marines wandered off alone after filling his canteen and was subsequently killed in a cleverly laid VC ambush just beyond our position. We suffered several wounded attempting to retrieve his body. It was probably a trade-off with the VC, but we'll never know for sure. There was no sign of them the next morning. They rarely leave any bodies or weapons on the battlefield.

As the operation wore on, we eventually slid back down to the rice paddy area. On the way, we retrieved the remains of others who had been killed in what had previously been inaccessible terrain. In addition, I went on a couple of daylight patrols through the hamlets, where I was able to speak to several of the local people. Finally, we flew by helo back to our battalion combat base. The VC had moved back into the area while we were gone and had made several contacts with other units.

Our big problem now was trying to keep the Đà nẵng airfield from being rocketed and keeping Highway #1 open to the north. The bridges were being blown almost at will, and I was becoming more involved since my job was resupplying all battalion units with the ammo, explosives, etc., necessary to keep the VC from hitting us. I think I was beginning to make my weight felt since the H & S (Headquarters and Service) Company Commander brought me a new government wristwatch! He, of course, had been one of my students at TBS. In fact, I've run into very few Lts that I did not instruct in TBS. Most come up and introduce themselves. It's a good feeling to be remembered, whether for good or bad!

I am still in the process of molding my initial impressions into some firm convictions about the war. One thing is for sure, though; it is far different from anything I have ever encountered. I am glad to be here, although I miss you all very much. It seems unfortunate that our country finds it so hard to sell this war. I think we need everyone we can get over here if we want to win.

As for living conditions, I sleep in the rear of my office . . . a wooden-floored, tin-roofed, screened-in, wooden hut about the size of a small single garage. I have not seen a toilet since I left Okinawa and have only had hot water one night while at the Division CP and some that I heated in the field once for shaving after three days' growth. Our water comes from 5-gallon cans that are refilled daily. Everything is done out in the open except sleeping. So far it has not bothered me a bit. The mess hall feeds hot chow, and I have not lost a pound, I'm sure. Of course, we eat C-rations when we are on an operation. I have not been sick yet, and I am taking a vitamin pill daily. We have some electricity, but not all the time.

4 NOV 67

An average day now will find me sitting at my field desk listening to Hawaiian music on Radio Vietnam with a cool breeze blowing through the mosquito screens. I finally had my first warm shower since arriving in country. LtCol Love has a small stall with a water drum fitted with an immersion burner that he offered to share. It works very well . . . in fact, it is outstanding! I love hot water! Last night I slept on a bed with actual sheets. I inherited the bed from Mac. I'm starting to enjoy this setup, but of course, I would give it up in a second to be out in the field with my own company.

LtCol Love surprised me this morning when he called and said that six-month fitness reports were due on captains and that although I had just arrived, he had written a special report on my performance during our last operation. I was flattered, to say the least. It was my first combat report and was very nearly all outstanding with a page-and-a-half written narrative! I hardly recognized the Marine being described! I guess my persistence in trying to command a company didn't hurt any!

My field phone has started to ring all day. Every day is the same. There is always something happening. Everything is a surprise to me, and I have to stop, research, and make some kind of decision. One morning, in the middle of a pouring rain, three Marines showed up, each stating they had been promised two large tents. I couldn't find anyone who knew how many tents we had or who had promised them . . . and things got worse as the day wore on!

On the other hand, Merrill, Wayne, all the Lts working for me (in communications, motor transport, and supply) and I were all at TBS at the same time. Additionally, LtCol Love was a Naval Academy graduate and had been one of my tactics instructors when I was a TBS student. I am continually amazed at how small and close our Corps is!

5 NOV 67

We had a typhoon warning yesterday, and I had everyone sandbag their tent roofs . . . but it finally changed course.

Most days now are spent working on reports. They seem to be due continuously. I also have started to work on my Vietnamese language with one of our interpreters. I have already forgotten so much.

7 NOV 67

Today I took a break from paperwork and saved it to do at night when it is normally more peaceful. I have a lot of research to do to get my office caught up with administrative requirements. So many new things are happening to me that I have a hard time remembering all the details. The other day I ventured out into a small Vietnamese hamlet and was invited to have tea with an older woman and her kids. The father had been assassinated by the VC. She was breastfeeding her baby while bathing another, and the third was going to the potty . . . all in what used to be a beautiful little villa with drapes still hanging around the family altar and shrine room, but now covered with mud, dust, and the decay of war.

One of the interesting things I did on Operation Knox and that LtCol Love mentioned in my Fitness Report was that I headed up a patrol of Otters (small tracked vehicles that can swim) to deliver some Vietnamese guides and interpreters to our companies. I'm afraid I didn't help our CAP (Civic Action Program) because, in order to get from one place to the next, I needed to drive through rice paddies and orchards, as well as swim down a river, to reach an old elevated French road that was partially destroyed. We spent two days and nights on patrol, and I ended up sleeping in cemeteries snuggled up next to old shrines for protection.

The Nam O bridge was blown up some time ago and is almost rebuilt again. It will be the only bridge still standing in our TAOR (tactical area of operations). The pressure is on us to keep it that way. The VC have vowed to blow it up again, and I have the responsibility to supply the company guarding it with everything needed to defend the bridge. I'll need to visit the bridge a lot.

Using my demolition experience from TBS, I have instituted the home-making of underwater explosives to keep VC divers away from the bridge pilings. Yesterday the VC ambushed two of our vehicles in the Hải Vân Pass just north of the bridge. That and a few other mishaps have kept me up several nights. As a result, I am staying very busy and the time is starting to go by more quickly.

My relief as the Logistics Officer arrived yesterday, Captain Jim Smith. I knew him in Iwakuni, Japan, where he worked in the 1st Marine Aircraft Wing intelligence section. He's not very happy since he also wanted a company . . . No surprise there! I tried to tell him that it is a good job, once you resign yourself to it. In fact, I told LtCol Love that now that I understand what's required in my job, I'm happy to stay in it until I leave on 9 Dec.

Tomorrow I will be the acting Commanding Officer for a parade ceremony to present awards to some of our Marines. One of the division generals will be coming to give the medals. The ceremony will start at 1 pm, and I need to have the parade ground ready before then. Maj Bill Shea (from TBS) is the Logistics Officer of the 7th Engineer Battalion and will provide the equipment needed to get the job done . . . thank goodness.

10 NOV 67 —*Marine Corps Birthday*

It seems that our battalion has been sadly lacking in electrical capability since arriving in Đà nẵng. During the last two weeks, I have researched the problem and inquired for possible solutions, much as we were trained to do at AWS (Amphibious Warfare School). Although there is a certain romantic value in writing personal letters by candlelight each night, it is a challenge trying to read maps and coordinate critical tactical situations under the same conditions. Therefore, as the Battalion Logistics Officer, I resolved to rectify the situation and devised a plan.

The day before yesterday, I began making arrangements to replace our small, tired generator. I coordinated with Maj Shea in our Engineer Battalion, who agreed to have a long flatbed semi-truck and driver standing by when needed. Next, I formed a small task force by first asking one of my former Lts from TBS, Jim McClung, to go along as my assistant. I then asked one of my logistics Marines, who was a qualified forklift driver, and two others, one of whom was the best generator mechanic in the battalion, to come along as guards.

The next night, at 7 pm, we borrowed a Jeep, picked up the flatbed truck, and headed toward Đà nẵng. I had told LtCol Love where I was going but left out all the details. I had my .45 caliber pistol and carried a shotgun. All other Marines were armed with M-16 rifles. The objective was a US Air Force installation close to the airfield that I had scouted earlier, where I had spotted a parking lot full of generators! However, it was fenced in with floodlights and a walking sentry.

Upon arrival, we staged the truck down the road, drove through the open gate in our Jeep, and jumped out. I carried the shotgun over my shoulder, quickly surveyed the area, and saw no one other than a young sentry, an Air Force sergeant. I approached him immediately and told him we were there to pick up our generator. Of course, he had no idea who we were or why we were there, only that I was a Marine Captain!

After the young sergeant recovered from his shock, he said that no one would be back in to work until much later and asked if I had my paperwork. I told him it had been filled out earlier and was probably in their office and that we were in a hurry! He then asked if we knew which generator to pick up. I said of course and walked across the lot with him and picked out the largest generator I could find, looked down at the serial number, read it out loud, and told him, "This is it. Where is your forklift to put it on our truck?" Our young sentry went into shock again and was incoherent at this point! Not knowing where to look, we flagged down an AF policeman driving by and asked him if he could help. He said he could and quickly led us to where some forklifts were parked, about a mile away. We found a large one, had our Marine forklift driver start it, and we were soon headed back down the road with the forklift following. The forklift was monstrous since we had selected a heavy generator to run our entire camp!

Once again, we descended on the young sentry, and while he was answering questions about the generator, we drove in the flatbed truck and forklift. The generator was loaded quickly onto the truck, tied down by my Marine guards, and off they went! We parked the forklift, and I thanked the sentry for his help. His parting comment as we sped out the gate was, "I hope it works OK for you, sir," to which my lieutenant calmly retorted, "If it doesn't, we'll bring it back!"

By midnight, as 10 Nov arrived, the sky-blue, 60-kW, 4800-lb. AF generator had been delivered to our camp, had turned Marine green and had its own new serial number! After it was hooked up, we asked LtCol Love to come down and officially throw the switch. We had a ceremony and took a picture. Happy Birthday, 2nd Battalion!

I cannot justify what I did unless you believe the end justifies the means, but many happy Marines were eating ice cream with their birthday cake the next day!

12 NOV 67

I was promoted to major at 4 pm today and had to ask Maj Shea to lend me a set of his gold major leaves since there is no place to buy them around here.

This was my final day in logistics. Jim will have to deal with all those challenges from now on. I attended church this morning and will start helping Wayne as the Assistant Operations Officer until I leave for Sài gòn next month. It was my turn in the operations center last night and the night before was our Marine Corps Birthday celebration . . . with lights run by our new generator! Now I need some sleep!

I was able to attend church almost every Sunday which gave me much spiritual strength. We always prayed for those who had been or would be hurt or killed . . . on both sides.

14 NOV 67

It has rained for three straight days. It isn't continuous, but when it starts, it really pours! It has had little effect on me, though, since I'm working in a bunker most of the time. Yesterday, however, several of us drove through the Hải Vân Pass, just north of Đà nẵng along Highway 1. We checked out all of our previous ambush sites and combat bases. Today Wayne and I drove over to another previous combat base and saw that it was completely surrounded by flooded rice paddies. I really enjoy getting out into the countryside and seeing everything, especially the people. I am communicating in Vietnamese better all the time.

My wetting down (promotion) party was last night at our small club. It costs me $70 and would have been more, except the bartender closed my bill out at midnight and charged the rest to the club (I had known the bartender in Iwakuni). The party lasted until 3 am with only the chaplain, LtCol Love, and me left! I was the only sober one, having had three cokes all night. We sang every song that LtCol Love could remember from the Academy and the Marine Corps, and every hymn the chaplain could remember. It was fun!

15 NOV 67

Today, with LtCol Love and Jim, I drove through the Hải Vân pass again on the way to Phú Lộc, which is a district Hq for the ARVN (Vietnamese Army). Phú Lộc was north of Đà nẵng along Highway 1. The US Army advisor there was a classmate back in the MATA school, so we compared notes while we ate lunch with his counterpart, an ARVN major and his officers. We had small tortillas, sausage balls with garlic, and some meatloaf with a beer to drink. I am still well except for a headache!

The drive there and back was as pretty as any I can remember anywhere. The beaches down below compared with my memory of the French Riviera back in 1958, where we spent some time on a midshipman cruise. The road reminded me of the Japanese roads where I used to ride my motorcycle north of Iwakuni. There were old French bunkers and a fort at the top of the mountain. Sometimes it was hard to remember that I had a loaded shotgun across my lap with my thumb on the safety! Unfortunately, we must be ready for ambushes since the road is very narrow and winding.

Yet another picture of this war can be seen driving down Highway #1, the main north/south road in South Vietnam, only one-and-a-half lanes with potholes everywhere, every bridge either destroyed or being repaired, a railroad track with every bridge blown up and burned up boxcars laying along-side, a line of power line poles, stretching into the distance with no power lines attached, and old men and women in almost every hamlet with peg legs and/or missing arms.

Add to this the bare-bottom little kids in the fields, men and women relieving themselves unashamedly along the roadside, old women with red betel-nut juice running down from the corner of their mouths, their teeth coated with a shiny black substance for beauty, and in the background . . . the bombed-out structures and cemeteries. This is what has happened to Vietnam; this is what Vietnam has become.

The Commanding General of the 3rd Marine Division was killed yesterday in a helicopter crash.

We would find out later that it was due to friendly fire and that Maj Bob Crabtree was aboard and also killed. I had relieved Bob at TBS as I returned home from Japan and he was reassigned to HQMC to be our infantry monitor. He found a way to send me to parachute jump school at Ft Benning, Georgia, during my Christmas leave in 1965.

Herb Hawkins is now the aide to the Commanding General of III MAF (Marine Amphibious Force), the senior Marine Hq in-country. Wayne and I will try to visit Herb before I depart the battalion.

17 NOV 67

Today I played Operations Officer all day and in fact, was the senior man in the battalion for a while. Both LtCol Love and our Executive Officer were called to Division Hq over several crises that we have had since yesterday. Besides drafting the normal flow of letters, memos, etc., and controlling the tactical play, patrolling, etc., within the battalion . . . the phone and radios have hummed incessantly with questions from 7th Marines and Division. I loved it! There is something happening all the time. Too bad I can't be an operations officer for a while; I think I would like it.

Other things are happening, though, that upset me terribly. It concerns me that the slightest reported incident, whether true or not, between a Marine and the local Vietnamese causes us to have to prove the Marine innocent to higher Hq. I am having a lot of first-hand experience dealing with these people up the line, and it isn't fun! Tomorrow I will head to Phú Lộc and to the G Company combat base at Phụ Gia to do some investigating. There are Marine careers that hang in the balance.

In the midst of all this, it now takes at least a LtCol to bug me! It feels good to be another rung up the ladder.

Even though I complain about things over here from time to time, I still feel like we are making progress and I am glad to have the opportunity to participate.

18 NOV 67

Last night, during my last jaunt to the COC, we called for several artillery missions and had a few firefights, which resulted in a few VC KIA (killed in action) with weapons. Unfortunately, we lost another Marine in the process. This morning, early, our road sweep was ambushed just this side of Phú Lộc and we had several more NVA (North Vietnamese Army) soldiers KIA and recovered some of their weapons. I was up there later and saw the results. It certainly wasn't pretty. A 50-caliber machine gun really does a brutal job!

As I look back on these casualties, both friendly and enemy, I wonder why it didn't bother me more at the time. I wrote about them almost matter-of-factly. It wasn't because we didn't care. We did. I continued to pray for them and their families. Maybe part of the answer was that higher headquarters required daily reports on everything, including numbers of wounded and killed, both friendly and enemy. We were so busy documenting everything that often there wasn't time to be emotional. Another part of the answer was that death was an unfortunate but continuing part of this war. There would be a battle in a few months in which the unit I was advising would lose almost 200 killed and wounded in less than 48 hours . . . and you move on.

I finished up another urgent matter today and completed the report. We were able to clear the Marine Corps from an incident that had been committed by the Vietnamese.

Tomorrow Assistant Division Commander BGen (Brigadier General) La Hue will journey to our CP to inspect the area and be briefed. I guess he wants to check out the "famous" 2nd Battalion. We have had more action and results with one platoon the last few days than the 3rd Battalion has had with their entire operation down south!

Years later, I would be the Assistant Division Commander of this division at Camp Pendleton, California, on my first assignment as a newly promoted BGen.

I talked with Bill U'ren on the phone for a while today to coordinate some patrol activity. He is still the Operations Officer with the 3rd Battalion.

Bill would soon lose a leg to a Claymore mine booby trap and be evacuated back to the States. He would recover, go to law school, and later become a district attorney outside of San Francisco.

LtCol Love called about 1 am, and we talked until 2 am about an investigation that I'm working on. There was still much to do . . . So went another day in the COC.

19 NOV 67

I missed Sunday church for the first time since arriving in Vietnam. From 7:30 am until this afternoon I worked on the investigation. It keeps getting more and more involved and has reached serious proportions. The Company Commander involved had been one of my students at TBS. I will need to head out to G Company tomorrow with the colonel, which means going through Hai Vân pass again. I'll carry my shotgun.

I don't worry about getting hurt. I just keep saying my prayers. In this war, a person has little to say about when or how he might be hurt. Only God can control that.

20 NOV 67

I am still working on the investigation. The typist is banging away. We redid the whole thing again and hope to save ten Marine courts-martial!

Hard to believe today that 50 years ago our administrative clerks had to bang out reports on big metal typewriters using reams of paper. It's a wonder that we ever finished any!

21 NOV 67

Today was easy for a change since there was no activity and I had very little to do. It was hard to stay awake. I walked over to our little club and had a Coke this evening!

22 NOV 67

We had another patrol ambushed last night. I watched the medical evacuation helicopter from our COC bunker, which is located on a hill. The Marine was hit down by the Nam O bridge and was seriously wounded.

This afternoon I wrote up another incident concerning a young Marine, which again could have easily meant a court-martial. What a war we are fighting. I guess I am seeing just about every side of it except the part I wanted to see.

Last night two men jumped off the civilian ship "Phoenix" as the Vietnamese were towing it out of the Đà nẵng harbor. It was carrying American peace activists, who had visited National Liberation Front officials in Hanoi and delivered medical supplies. Marines from one of our companies picked up one of the men and whisked him into Division very fast! He was after publicity for his anti-war cause. What a mixed-up bunch of people.

I had no idea at the time how fast the tide of support for the war was waning.

My orders to report to MACV on 9 Dec arrived today. I plan to go down to the airfield on the 8th and get manifested with the Air Force so that I will have a reserved seat to Sài gòn on the 9th.

23 NOV 67

Wayne and I went down to III MAF Hq and talked with LtCol Hatch, Herb Hawkins, and Larry McLaughlin. It surely was good to see them again. They are living pretty high on the hog!

We all served together at TBS. In a few more weeks, LtCol Hatch would be killed in a helo crash.

Not much has happened today. One of our trucks was hit. No one hurt. It poured down rain all day.

24 NOV 67

The package arrived with my new "major" insignias. Thank you. Now I can return the ones I borrowed from Bill Shea.

The colonel gave me another investigation. I am really getting an insight into another side of this war. I hope these requirements are different in other commands. It will be a real pleasure to go somewhere and fight rather than have to appease higher Hq with paperwork all the time. I am still trying to figure out why the colonel is giving me all the investigations to write up. Maybe I'll find out when he writes my fitness report as I transfer to MACV.

Tonight, we made a run down to the Nam O bridge to check on the new lights that we had installed for better security at night. I had my shotgun ready as usual, but nothing happened. We did have an ARVN truck ambushed further down the road, and several people were hurt, but no Marines.

25 NOV 67

Last night I moved into a new hooch (small hut) with Wayne and Mac, next to LtCol Love's and we really fixed it up. It now is nicer than the Executive Officer's, and his jealousy is becoming evident!

My latest investigations are getting involved again. Tomorrow I will venture forth incognito—fat chance of that happening—into one of the villages and see what I can find out from the local people.

Chaplain Grubbs asked me to read the Scripture in church tomorrow *(I first met the chaplain in Iwakuni and had enjoyed his chapel services there)*. He is a good man. I'll read the scripture before I head out to the ville (village) to investigate.

26 NOV 67

I read the scripture in chapel this morning. I still enjoy going and singing, even without an organ or piano. Afterwards, I picked up an interpreter and roamed around out in the village until I had enough info to write the investigation.

It seems a little different being away from family this time. It may be because we are all in the same boat. Everyone here is separated from their family. During my year in Iwakuni, Japan, the Marines were all unaccompanied while the Navy had their families with them . . . big impact on morale!

We received the 1st Marine Division Christmas cards this week, and they are very nice. I will try to send as many as I can to family and friends.

27 NOV 67

It rained all day again. Mac was transferred to the 3rd battalion to be their Operations Officer, so Wayne and I have lots of room in our new hooch.

One of our companies was hit pretty hard by the VC last night and again today. They were part of Operation Foster, with LtCol Barnard's 3rd Battalion, and they ran into a real hornets' nest. It was hard for me to just sit here when I know how tough it must be for the Marines in contact with the enemy. I guess I might change my mind one day, but right now it is very hard. Yes, I am still working on investigations!

28 NOV 67

I wrote LtCol Leftwich today, whom I had known when he was a captain at the USNA and later with the 2nd Marines at Camp LeJeune, NC. I wanted to congratulate him on his promotion since he had written to me in Japan when I was promoted to captain.

LtCol Leftwich was awarded a Navy Cross as a VNMC advisor on his first Vietnam tour. He would later be killed on his second tour during a helo reconnaissance team extraction. Many in our Corps had believed he would one day be Commandant of the Marine Corps.

The monsoon season is fast approaching. The mountains close by have been covered with clouds for several days. Any future operations will be hampered by the weather for sure.

29 NOV 67

Although I have written of my concern about the way things are being dictated from senior commands, I don't think I will ever be disappointed in our Marine Corps. However, there are a few individuals that are disappointing from time to time . . . but I'm sure that is probably true of most places. I've even been disappointed in myself more than once. Sometimes it is very hard to keep going full bore all the time, but that's what Marines seem to do . . . most of them. So far, I have managed to keep going at a pretty strong pace. But I am ready now to head south and start my new job as an advisor. There is no doubt that the last three years of training at Quantico have been invaluable. I have finished the other investigations, and the colonel has accepted them. I have also written up a couple of other things. I'm just about written out!

Wayne and I plan to go over to 7th Marines in the morning and ask for guidance on a forthcoming operation. There has been none so far, which is nothing new! This is the other side of my frustration—no guidance vs. too much guidance! I will miss this op since I will head to Sài gòn next week before they finish, and once again I will start from scratch and see what new horizons lay ahead. If nothing else, the Marine Corps does teach us how to continually step into new and different situations and cope with them. We are supposed to be a specialist in everything we do, and if we're not, someone comes along that is . . . and off we go again.

2 DEC 67

I've spent the last two days writing an estimate for the proposed operation I mentioned earlier. LtCol Love said he was pleased with what I've done so far. I should be finished tomorrow so I can start packing to head south.

The estimate consisted of all the advantages and disadvantages of running the operation from every viewpoint . . . aviation, artillery, communications, supply, etc., from both the enemy and friendly side. It is exactly what we learned how to do back in AWS at Quantico before we were sent to Vietnam.

Our company just returned from their operation with the 3rd Battalion. They were chewed up badly. A new captain, who had just reported in, had taken over the company when the previous commander had been wounded. There seemed to have been some difficulty in coordination between our company and the 3rd Battalion Hq, and a lot of people ended up getting hurt.

The monsoons have arrived! It has been raining for three days and nights. The mud is building up. The weather is getting cooler but doesn't require a jacket yet. It does make for better sleeping.

4 DEC 67

LtCol Love has asked me to stay longer and has asked for my orders to be delayed! It all revolves around Operation Pitt, which is supposed to start tomorrow. The original word from Division was that they were going to accept some of the recommendations from our estimate, which included changing the operating area. That was Saturday evening. Today, Sunday, I slipped off to church and took communion, and by the time I returned, Division had changed their mind again, and we were back to the original operating area, plus sending two platoons immediately to search for a downed helicopter and an errant Hawk missile, which had been accidentally fired.

Later, the chopper search mission was canceled, since it was discovered that it actually had crashed two years ago! Meanwhile, the colonel and Wayne were on their way to Division carrying our final estimate for the operation that was supposed to start tomorrow, Monday morning.

I began to send out Warning Orders with the latest changes to our three companies that were available. Our other company was already committed to the earlier search mission . . . which was now canceled! Div then ordered us to have the search company stand by for pickup in 45 minutes to be returned to our battalion CP. I sent the order, but the Company Commander radioed me that he still had one platoon looking for the Hawk missile and could not make the deadline! I suggested that he reconsider and do it anyway. Now I sounded like higher Hq.

However, Division then canceled the helo pickup and ordered us to pick them up by truck tomorrow, Monday. But before we could cancel the helo lift, the first helo had already shown up and was loading. Division then canceled the truck pickup for tomorrow and approved the helo lift for the second time. At this point, the Company Commander requested to only send one platoon back by helo since some of his people were still moving by foot through the Hai Vân pass between our CP and his, having left before all the changes from Division began. So, with the choppers on the way for the second load, we aborted the mission. By this time, it was evident to me that the operation for tomorrow needed to be delayed. No kidding! Amazingly enough, we then received word from Div that Op Pitt was in fact delayed! If you understood any of this, you are one of the few!

At this point, LtCol Love and Wayne returned from Division with the latest word! Division had decided to accept our recommended area for the operation after all, and we would jump off Tuesday morning. Wayne and I wrote the new operation order last night, Sunday, and made copies this morning, Monday. We then issued new Warning Orders, arranged for everything else that needed arranging and prepared for the final briefing for all commanders. Then 7th Marines entered the fray and issued a Fragmentary Order to us with a different mission . . . Unbelievable!

Well, we appreciated their effort, but we just filed it for future reference and went ahead with our final briefing! The rest of today has been spent in ironing out the last few wrinkles, picking up our attached units, and issuing the necessary equipment and supplies. I think it will be a good operation. My only regret is that I can't go. Someone needs to stay back and run the COC (combat operations center), plus I will be headed south before they get back.

Last night LtCol Love called me over to their little club and presented me with a battalion plaque with my name on it for my short period of service with them . . . very nice. I thanked them and returned to the COC and finished the operation order about 1 am. It was as easy as some of our assignments at AWS. I'm appreciating that school more and more.

We picked up a company from the 3rd Battalion today to help patrol our section of the rocket belt around Đà nẵng (to keep the bad guys from firing rockets into the airfield) while our battalion is on the operation. I don't foresee any difficulties.

6 DEC 67

With no word to the contrary, I expect to leave Friday and be in Sài gòn by the 9th as originally ordered . . . but I do feel obligated to stay here until the last minute.

This operation has begun just like our last one, Operation Knox . . . no contact with the enemy. It's been pretty easy back here in the COC. Once things are organized, everything flows smoothly until something unexpected happens!

Tomorrow I must pack and turn in my shotgun. I will be busy until I leave for Sài gòn.

3

I finally made it to Sài gòn, but it was a rat race trying to leave the battalion. Operation Pitt is still going on with even more changes thrown in. I was up until 1 am this morning trying to clarify things. Before that, I was invited back to our little club to say goodbye by those not on the operation, and it cost me $20 to buy everyone a round! I had a good time in that battalion but am also really impressed with what I've seen here in Sài gòn.

I left this morning from the Air Force side of the Đà nẵng airfield (only a block from where we found the generator that I wrote about earlier). The 11 am flight was booked solid, but I had gotten to know the Marine Gunny, who was the liaison staff NCO (non-commissioned officer) and behold, I was added to the flight! It was then delayed for an hour, but I eventually got here. It only took an hour and fifteen minutes. When I arrived in Sài gòn at the Tân Sơn Nhứt airfield, it was a madhouse! I finally found a colonel whom I remembered from a visit with LtCol Hatch back at the 1st Division Hq in Đà nẵng. He was here for a briefing and took me to the III MAF liaison office. I called the Marine Advisory Unit (MAU) from there, and it's been smooth sailing since.

Captain John Hainsworth, the Administrative Officer, picked me up in a Jeep that looked like it had been spit-shined! Our Jeeps in Đà nẵng were covered with mud and barely running when I left. John was wearing a set of tiger striped utilities and green beret . . . quite a contrast to my old faded jungle utilities. *In a couple of months, John would be sent to help me as an assistant advisor during the Tết Offensive.* John drove me to the MAU, I reported in, and found out that I will be the senior advisor to the 4th Battalion, VNMC. Maj Bob Hamilton (from TBS) has the job right now but will head home shortly.

Sadly, Bob would pass away years later from having had contact with Agent Orange earlier in his Vietnam tour. Agent Orange was a strong defoliant dropped from aircraft in Vietnam to strip the foliage from tall trees so that the enemy could be detected below. Unfortunately, it was later found that direct exposure to it caused many to develop cancer.

I've already met and talked with Colonel Michael, the Senior Marine Advisor. The other advisors who happen to be in town, all Captains, took me to dinner and a nightclub for the evening. What a change of scenery in the last 24 hours! Curfew was at midnight, so I'm now checked into a small hotel in the middle of Sài gòn for a couple of days of briefings. Then I report to Task Force A (one of the two higher Hq for the VNMC battalions) on the 10th as an assistant advisor until I relieve Bob at the 4th Battalion.

The Vietnamese Marine Corps, Thủy quân lục chiến (TQLC) in Vietnamese, was formed in 1954 starting with one infantry battalion and one US Marine advisor. When I arrived in 1967, they had grown to six infantry battalions, two artillery battalions, two Task Force headquarters, and the necessary supporting units. Marine advisors were assigned to each unit. After I left, they added three more infantry battalions and another task force headquarters, now called a Brigade Headquarters, and could operate as a Division. The TQLC were considered an elite organization, as were the ARVN Airborne units, and were only filled with volunteers. Most of the TQLC officers would attend TBS and/or AWS early in their career. Both the Vietnamese Marine and Airborne units were used as a national reserve strike force and were routinely committed throughout the country.

After my disappointment up north, I can hardly believe it is working out so well down here. I talked to Capt Gene Gardner on the phone today, and he said that he would stop by tomorrow.

Gene was currently the senior advisor to the 6th Battalion. He had graduated from the USNA in 1960, and we served together at

TBS. His wife Phyllis and children were neighbors in Woodbridge and, similar to Charlie's family, would end up being neighbors again and remain friends through the years. Unfortunately, after retiring, Gene too eventually died from Agent Orange exposure.

I'm in a single room with a view of the city, private hot water shower and bath, a real bed with a mattress, and a real toilet that flushes!

This would all be short-lived, and soon, even the Đà nẵng amenities would seem like a treat!

9 DEC 67

It was wonderful to shower and shave with hot water this morning without being in the wind and rain. I feel like I'm on R&R (Rest and Recreation). Gene dropped by this afternoon, and we went out on the town for a little while. I had a lobster dinner last night and French onion soup with chateaubriand tonight. They were both out of this world! Hard to believe there is a war going on!

But in less than two months, I would be landing again at Ton Son Nhut . . . this time under fire with the 4th VNMC Battalion as we fought our way across town during the Tết Offensive.

Gene said he had accidentally shot one of his battalion Marines in the leg during a night ambush and had left the battalion for now until they can sort out what happened! Seems the young Marine was in the wrong place at the wrong time. Hope it is resolved soon.

Today I processed my records and was briefed on regulations for the city. I found out that I've already broken most of them! I guess the Marine advisors have decided to live dangerously here in the city! Two more days of briefings and I'll be heading up country to the 4th Battalion. I can hardly wait.

10 DEC 67

I need to get out of Sài gòn! This is like being in the States. I'm eating myself broke! Tonight, I grilled steaks with the other advisors at the Splendid Hotel, which is where many of the US military personnel live full time. Sài gòn is like many other big cities except it's a little more dangerous! There are civilians everywhere, including many American women. I think they must be part of the US Embassy and other government agencies.

The classes today were nothing to get excited about. Tomorrow will no doubt be worse. We were given most of this info back in the MATA school at Fort Bragg.

I wasn't surprised at the choice for our new Marine Commandant. I think it was a good move for our Corps. I've heard Gen Chapman speak and I'm impressed. He is forward-thinking and is pushing for all officers to have computer training.

11 DEC 67 —*written from the Ambassador Hotel in Sài gòn*

I found out today that the 4th Battalion is home-based in Vũng Tàu, a beautiful resort town on the east coast not far from here and considered to be an R&R center for the rest of the Vietnamese, on both sides! However, right now the battalion is operating in Bồng Son, which is up in II Corps. SVN is divided into four tactical Corps areas, with an ARVN General in charge of each one. Sài gòn and Vũng Tàu are in III Corps and Đà nẵng is in I Corps.

I have moved from my single room in the Koehler Compound to the Ambassador Hotel, where I have an air-conditioned suite, with two bedrooms and a shared bathroom. It will be temporary until I leave for the 4th Battalion. I'm hoping to end up with a room at the Splendid Hotel whenever I'm back in Sài gòn, which is where Gene stays when he is not with his battalion.

Tomorrow the MAU staff will start briefing me, and I will be issued my Vietnamese camouflaged utilities (cammies) and gear for the field. I've been wearing the standard issue solid green jungle utilities since I arrived in Vietnam. The jungle utilities are much lighter and dry faster than the ones we wore back in the states.

12 DEC 67

Today I was issued my field gear and cammies. This gear is much newer than what we had up north. Tomorrow I'll be issued my green beret and tiger striped utilities with the red 4th Battalion name patch sewn on the jacket. These utilities are more like a dress uniform for the VNMC. Each of the six battalions has a different colored name tag. Ours is red. I've also been issued an M-16 rifle instead of a .45 caliber pistol.

Just found out that the VNMC Chief of Staff is Col Bùi The Laan, who lived across the hall from me when we were students going through TBS. Small world.

I did a very foolish thing as I left Đà nẵng. I forgot to pick up my military pay record! I called and asked Division Hq to mail it down here, but who knows when it will arrive. Needless to say, I'm out of money and had to borrow from the Advisor slush fund so I can buy food.

13 DEC 67

My last day in Sài gòn was uneventful. I finally have my new cammies with red name tag and other assorted goodies, and my little green beret fits nicely. I think I must look like a Christmas tree! I guess I'm now an official Cố vấn (VNMC term for their advisors).

Captain Harry Shane, advisor to the VNMC training center, took me there today and I fired my M-16 until I was comfortable, and played with some explosives and napalm for defensive measures. Driving back and forth through half of Sài gòn with no problems gives a false sense of security until you realize that there are VC all around just waiting for an opportunity to strike.

I'm glad I'm not staying in Sài gòn since it appears that the many US civilians in town drawing COLA (cost of living allowance) extra dollars have jacked up the cost for the rest of us. I don't think I saw this many US civilians in Tokyo during the 1964 Olympics!

The city is beginning to take on new aspects as I wander through it more and more. I see the same people on the outskirts that I saw up north . . . little kids with nothing on, old ladies with betel-nut spittle running out the corner of their mouths, garbage and trash thrown everywhere, all ages and genders relieving themselves in public, and traffic racing all over. Most of the native women and girls wear black baggy trousers and some sort of colored blouse. The men wear anything they can find.

The hotels in town are typically French and remind me a little of those on the French Riviera. However, there is no glamour left on those being used to house our military. The tiny bathroom fixtures and small open central elevators are the main reminders on the inside, while the outside architecture readily shows the French influence.

Gene went back to the 6th Battalion today, and I've checked out of my hotel since it was only temporary.

16 DEC 67—*written from TF A, VNMC CP, Bồng Sơn*

My plane was eight hours late leaving Tân Sơn Nhứt. It was a C-110 (small transport aircraft) with no seats! It took an hour to get to Quy Nhơn where we landed at 1 am. I ended up sleeping in the terminal and finally hitched a ride on an Army Caribou aircraft about 10:30, which landed first at An Khe and later, at LZ English in the middle of an Army complex. No one there had ever heard of the 4th Battalion, VNMC, so I wandered around until I found a couple of Army officers, who fed me and gave me a ride just south of Bồng Sơn. From there I hitchhiked about ten miles down Highway 1 with an Army advisor until I finally saw Vietnamese tiger suits with red name tags. At last, the 4th Battalion!

It didn't take much longer to locate Bob Hamilton, and he took me to Task Force (TF) A. It was good to see friends again. The Vietnamese Assistant TF Commander is Maj Luong from my AWS class. The Quantico connections continue! We are living in a bunker with all of our radios connecting us to the rest of our world. Maj Tom Ward (*AWS, and Woodbridge neighbor*) and Capt Ron Ray are with the 3rd Battalion and are also located here. Maj Tim Budd and 1st Lt Dick Perry are the TF advisors. (*Tim also would later be claimed by Agent Orange.*) The 4th Battalion is just north of here, and I will join them on 1 Jan.

I'm scheduled to go on a small operation with Tom in a few days to get the feel of how an advisor interfaces with his counterpart. So far, I'm liking it. The food is good, and I've figured out how to squat over a hole in the ground . . . very different from my experience in

Vietnam to date! The weather is cool here like it was up north, and I'm hoping we head south before too long so I can warm up again. I'm back to cold showers . . . an old metal drum that we stand under and turn on the faucet. I don't like that part! But don't get me wrong, I'm enjoying the job. I feel like this is the best place to be in this kind of war. The Vietnamese must win the war if it is to be won, not the US Marine Corps, and I would like to think I might be able to speed up the victory for them by helping when they need me. Right now, so many new things are happening compared to the way things were done in the 1st Marine Division that it will take me a while to settle in.

18 DEC 67

The radios are on 24 hours a day and must be monitored by us. We trade off, and it's not too bad. The difference is that we had radio operators up north. But in the bunker, WE are the radio operators. It's been raining all day, and it's cold. The space blanket and poncho liner are life savers for me!

I went on a helicopter reconnaissance of the area this morning and observed the 4th Battalion operating with some US Army Calvary units. The Army owns all the helos around here but seems happy to share.

Bob's assistant advisor, 1st Lt Tony Zinni, is being medically evacuated this evening for hepatitis. I talked with him today, and I think he will be okay but will probably be in the hospital for at least a month. He has lost a lot of weight. I'm guessing I'll move over to the 4th Battalion sooner now to help Bob.

Tony would recover and return for a tour up north with the US Marines. Years later we would serve together as colonels at HQMC and he would go on to be promoted to General and become the Commander in Chief of Central Command.

20 DEC 67—*written from the 4th Battalion, VNMC CP, Bồng Sơn*

I moved to the 4th Battalion yesterday. I like this much better than living with the task force advisors. Bob and I have a broken-down, leaky bunker to ourselves with cots and mosquito nets. There is no electricity and no shower or bathroom facilities. We get our water from a stream below and of course, have to boil it. Our little camp looks more like it could host a band of roving gypsies or hobos than a military unit. There is an Army artillery outfit not far away that has much better facilities, but I wouldn't feel right using them when the Vietnamese can't.

I've decided to try to eat everything the Vietnamese eat rather than be picky and hungry. They normally eat twice a day . . . always rice and soup, with some kind of meat (not much) and vegetable, depending on what's available close by . . . and afterward, a cup of tea. It's easy to fill up on the rice, so I don't ever feel hungry. My counterpart is from North Vietnam, and they like meat and soy sauce. So do I! Oh, the cost per day for my chow is about 60 cents!

I have a bodyguard, called a "cowboy," who watches out for me and fixes all my meals. His name is Chiến. And I have another Vietnamese Marine named Mạnh, who carries my radio, drives my Jeep when we are traveling, and stays close by. Together they make sure I have a place to sleep, food to eat, and carry any personal gear that I need. Neither speaks English, but we get along just fine with my beginning Vietnamese.

So far, the Vietnamese seem to like me. They appreciate that I have already spent time with US Marines in I Corps and that I'm a major. My counterpart will be Capt Voung after Bob departs. All the company commanders have been to TBS, and Capt V attended the Army Infantry School at Fort Benning, Georgia, which should prove very helpful.

Yesterday morning Tom and I drove over to the US Army 2nd Brigade to coordinate, and I met LtCol Love, US Army . . . the brother of my battalion commander in Đà nẵng. This LtCol Love graduated from West Point.

This morning about 6:30, the Battalion Executive Officer and I went on a small operation with three companies. Bob stayed back with the Battalion Commander, Captain Vuong. We took a few sniper rounds, picked up one VC suspect, and had one friendly KIA due to an accident. I called in some Army helos for some reconnaissance, but that was about it. My only disappointment happened in one of the small hamlets we walked through. I stopped to talk with a few kids, and the baby with them started to cry as soon as I smiled! I thought about that for a long time. Was I that scary, or was this just another face of the war?

The 3rd and 4th Battalions have had a few VC KIA every day since I arrived, and this morning, the 3rd Battalion had a whole bunch more and captured their weapons.

This sounds so crude now, but when I originally wrote it, it was part of our mission of trying to pacify the hamlets by eliminating the threat to their otherwise peaceful existence. What we were starting to realize, though, was that this wasn't working. Many of the VC were, in fact, the men of the village, so we were destroying families. And unless we were there full time, the VC would return and punish any that did not support them.

21 DEC 67

My life is easy for now. The sun is out and hot. I'm happy and warm again! Most of our companies are committed to road and bridge security. Hoping for an operation soon.

I'm improving with the chopsticks. I've not seen anyone eating with knives and forks outside of the larger towns.

22 DEC 67

Bob and I are down to one candle for writing at night, but so far it is sufficient. We also hooked up a small six-inch Christmas tree to one of our radio batteries and can also tune in to a station playing Christmas music. Our bunker is half open, and with the clear sky tonight, we can see the stars, but reality quickly sets in when our mortars occasionally kick out a few rounds and the Army twin 40mm guns start popping tracers across the rice paddies below.

We are situated on a small hill and can see as far as the hills to the west. The Đầm Trà Ổ lake is to our east and Highway 1 is to our west.

Bob and I attended church services earlier today down where the Army artillery unit is located.

23 DEC 67

I wandered around today and watched how our meals were prepared. The vegetables are cut up with a pocket knife and dumped into a metal helmet filled with water, which is then hung over an open fire inside a small three-sided hovel about the size of a doghouse. The chicken, other meat, or fish is then hacked apart with a bayonet, cleaned, and fried in a pan over the same fire. Lots of pepper and soy sauce are used. The rice is cooked in an old ammo (ammunition) can over the fire. It is always fluffy and dry. It amazes me that the food is so good!

24 DEC 67

We have our Christmas candle burning and little tree sparkling. We are observing a ceasefire starting today, and the quiet is very eerie. Occasionally an illumination round will burst in the sky. It has rained all day. I wonder if the VC will try to take advantage of the ceasefire?

My Christmas Eve dinner was rice, fried pork, string beans, and melon soup. I'm hoping my taste for rice will last . . . if not, I'm going to be hungry!

26 DEC 67

Christmas passed, and it is one I shall not soon forget. The most beautiful thing happened Christmas Eve night. After feeling sorry for myself too long, I drifted off to sleep with my radio close by (battalion advisors sleep with their radios at night). Sometime later I woke up suddenly, thinking I had either dreamed or was hearing a strange noise. Not being sure whether it was a dream or my radio, I strained to listen. It wasn't coming from my radio, and it began to sound like music. In fact, it was beginning to sound like "Silent Night." I went outside the bunker, and the music became louder. I wondered if the angels were serenading us or if I was hallucinating.

Then I heard the familiar whop—whop—whop of helicopter rotor blades. The Army had sent their psychological warfare helo with loudspeakers to fly over all of the outlying combat posts playing Christmas songs! What a wonderful Christmas Eve surprise. On Christmas Day the same helo flew over again and wished us Merry Christmas over our radio frequency. The Christmas spirit was alive and well, even over here, thanks to the US Army!

Also, yesterday, the Army unit at the bottom of the hill invited Bob and me to a holiday meal. This time, I went. Their mess hall cooks had been up all night and had fixed a wonderful spread. We had turkey, gravy, mashed potatoes, sweet potatoes, shrimp cocktail, egg nog, cranberry sauce, rolls, strawberry shortcake, pumpkin pie, mincemeat pie, and fruitcake. I remembered how to use a fork and ate too much. I came very close to getting sick! But it was delicious.

The truce ended at 6 pm today and at 6:01 there were artillery rounds in the air again. It sounded like we were trying to make up for lost time. However, there were no incidents during the truce.

We jumped off this morning at 3:30 on a three-company operation along the Đầm Trà Ổ lake and picked up 18 suspects which I'm sure are VC. The village has many more VC hiding in it that we missed, but we will pick them up next time. We accidentally injured a small boy with a stray round. He wasn't seriously hurt but I medevaced him aboard a helo anyway. He had such a pitiful look on his face. I hope he can forgive us. If not, he probably will end up wearing black pajamas and being another VC. What kind of war is this when the villagers must live at the mercy of whoever controls the night?

Before we left, one of the village women offered me a bowl of spiced noodles, shrimp, and herbs. That was a first! Unfortunately, the spices were too hot for me.

28 DEC 67

Bob leaves tomorrow, and I am officially now the senior advisor to the 4th Battalion, VNMC . . . or the senior Cố vấn, to use the Vietnamese term. We had another small one-company operation start yesterday. Maj Budd at TF A sent one of his assistant advisors to be with that company since I needed to stay back with the battalion commander.

Gunnery Sergeant Mobley became my assistant and will probably stay until another officer checks in to the MAU. He is one of only five enlisted Marines assigned to the MAU. If first impressions are lasting, he will work out fine.

I went up in the Army Command and Communications (C&C) helo this morning and watched Gunny Mobley and our company being helo-lifted into their area of operations. All went well.

I returned in time to join the rest of the battalion in saying goodbye to Bob.

It was quite a party with TF A Hq folks also there. Most of the Vietnamese officers have been to school in the states and somehow developed a taste for scotch, but they mix Coke with it. Uhggg! I sat next to Tom and traded my scotch for his cups of Coke, hoping the Vietnamese would not notice. But they finally caught on and vowed to teach me how to drink scotch! We will see.

It wasn't until I retired that I developed a taste for single malt scotch . . . but certainly not with Coke!

My use of chopsticks continues to improve. My only difficulty is with fish . . . learning how to twist the meat off of the bones. The Vietnamese don't use their fingers when eating.

29 DEC 67

My greatest difficulty at present is trying to keep track of the date. I always know the time, but there is no ready reference for the date. My only outside communication is my tactical radio and your letters, which arrive on an irregular basis, and I feel silly asking for the date over a radio reserved for fighting the war.

There were 50 VC reported to have been in the village before our company arrived yesterday. That will make me feel a little uneasy tonight in my bunker alone, now that Bob has left. I have my tactical radio of course, and the Vietnamese Marines are around for security, but this will be the first time that I will be the only American here on our hilltop. I'll try to listen to Armed Forces Radio or Voice of America tonight if I can reach them with my little battery-operated radio.

Right now, I'm being shocked back into reality by the constant pounding of mortar and artillery shells exploding in the valleys and distant hills around us. Occasionally a lone rat will dart across the floor looking for something to eat. All of this reminds me of how much I miss the comforts of home, but the more I talk with the Vietnamese officers, the more I realize how isolated our country seems to be from the discomforts of the rest of the world. I hope that I can be part of the solution to help the VNMC lessen the discomfort for their country.

Unfortunately, for many reasons much clearer now than then, we would never finish the job.

30 DEC 67

For lunch, we had rice again, along with spiced shrimp. The heads and tails were chopped off, but we ate the rest with shells left on. Our soup was a spinach-like vegetable boiled in a canteen cup of water. It was all hot coming directly off an open fire and really tasted good as the weather has started to get colder. We ate everything using chopsticks, of course, and drank the soup.

31 DEC 67

The end of another year has arrived for us, but not the Vietnamese.

Their celebration would come a month later, and it would be a shock!

We had another shooting incident where an Army soldier, driving down Highway #1 in a Jeep, took a potshot at one of our Vietnamese Marines. Apparently, this has been happening about once a week. I'm concerned that our Marines may start firing back . . . and I wouldn't blame them. Today when it happened, I got there too late to stop the Jeep but called ahead to TF A, and Tom ran down and stopped the first Army Jeep he saw. It wasn't the right Jeep, but Tom passed the word about our concern. Hope this was enough to stop the random shooting.

My cowboy and his friends have just invited me to their hooch for a little snake and bác sĩ để (Vietnamese liquor). I couldn't turn them down. The snake came from the Army unit across the road. The unit commander's brother had gone through the MATA course with me, was a good friend, and was a '59 graduate from West Point. I had invited him over for a beer earlier after I had bought some for my Gunny. These few moments of levity keep me going!

The battalion Operations Officer just brought me a small album for my family pictures. He wouldn't let me pay him. So nice!

We had cabbage soup tonight with fried pork, fried white beanstalks, with soy sauce and hot red peppers. The peppers are about ¾" and very hot! I wasn't the only one with tears in my eyes. Of course, we finished with steaming rice.

I'll stay up until midnight and wish TF A "happy new year" over the radio.

1 JAN 68

Happy New Year! I didn't go to church yesterday because the Army chaplain wasn't here. I really miss that time each week.

Tonight, after chow we had another accidental shooting with an M-16. I called the Army for a medevac, and they were here in 10 minutes and saved our young Marine's life. He had been shot through the abdomen. It was bad.

It has been raining for two days, and it is becoming muddy and cold. The wind whistles through my bunker which has only three sides with no heater.

I'm listening to Armed Forces Radio, and Bob Hope is in Vietnam somewhere, but not anywhere close to us.

I was never in a place where I could watch Bob Hope in Vietnam but did watch him years later in 29 Palms, California. I did stay in a hotel later in Bangkok where Hope would spend the night when he performed in Vietnam.

I was able to get the Vietnamese to give me a haircut today with manual clippers . . . the first since leaving Sài gòn.

The Gunny was able to scrounge a piece of equipment from the

Army that could prove very useful . . . a five-gallon water can with a nozzle. If it ever warms up, we will have a shower.

2 JAN 68

The young Vietnamese Marine that we medevaced last night died at 2 am. More prayers.

This afternoon our nearby Army unit had enemy contact over by the lake, where we were last week. They used helos and tracked vehicles and managed to get themselves in a lot of trouble. I watched it through my binoculars as three of their helos were shot down. I monitored their radio, and it sounded like I was listening to young lieutenants back at TBS! Very sad. Many unnecessary casualties. What a bag of worms! They finally asked after dark if we could help. We did, and the VC backed off and disappeared. Maybe there's a reason why the VC attacked the Army and not the Marines!

I'm not trying to judge but only making a comment based on my limited observation and experience.

I heard today that Gene's 6th Battalion may be relieving us at the end of the month. I need to tell him that I don't think my bunker will last that long! I think the rains and wind will have leveled it by then!

3 JAN 68

The radio news from the Army contact I mentioned yesterday was not accurate. It mentioned 50 VC KIA. It was only 15. I was monitoring their radio. This is part of my discomfort with the pressure from above for numbers. We can't win the war like this. There has to be a better way.

I had a company standing by to help the Army, but my own TF A never committed it. This morning they denied any knowledge. Wow! I need to grow up fast if I'm going to survive this situation. I requested an artillery mission about 3 am, which took over five minutes . . . this is not good! Things will work out. They always do, but I'm a little anxious right now.

We have a new operation coming up on the 5th. Capt Vuong

and I are flying down to Quy Nhon tomorrow to be briefed. I'm hoping the whole battalion will be committed so I can go also.

The guns continue to pound every night around here. Just heard that our 1st and 2nd Battalions were hit down south somewhere during the truce. There were many casualties on both sides. The advisors were okay.

4 JAN 68

I've been busy today. This morning I flew south to Quy Nhon for a briefing and ran into another Army advisor that I knew from the MATA course. Our battalion jumps off tomorrow to the west by helo for three to five days. Tom's 5th Battalion will walk in. We will be on the hilltops and it will be cold. The Army and ARVN will be on the low ground. I also heard that the Army found another 100 VC bodies from the operation I described earlier . . . and that one of the helos that was shot down had a US Marine LtCol observer from III MAF aboard. More prayers.

Later I would confirm that my Marine friend, LtCol Hatch, died from burns suffered in that crash. I can remember seeing the smoke when the helo crashed.

I've been working out some details for our operation but think I'm ready to go now. It will be good to start operating again.

8 JAN 68

While writing this letter about our operation, I was interrupted by another urgent medevac request. One of our Marines had just been severely wounded in the head by accidentally tripping a booby-trap. We were able to put him on the helicopter in less than 10 minutes.

Not much activity on our operation. We helo-lifted into the hills west of our CP and walked for three days. It turned out to be a walk in the sun. This morning we walked back to our CP. Not very exciting, but that was a good thing! All we had to eat was the rice with fried pork fat that we carried with us. I'm learning to enjoy whatever Chién fixes for me. We needed to fly in water by helo each day, which was critical, but I was able to exist easily with less than a full canteen per day.

One new thing I discovered on this operation, and it surprised me, was that the Vietnamese do not have the stamina to operate like this for more than a couple of days without rest. Even my counterpart Captain Vuong had to stop, drink water, and rest time after time . . . and he only carries a pistol and canteen, as do I. Our cowboys carry everything else that we might need. Perhaps it is their smaller body structure and poor diet.

Or maybe it had to do with the fact that they had been doing this week after month after year without seeing an end in sight.

I'm still holding up with no physical problems, and I'm grateful. The second night I did 50 push-ups to check my strength and endurance . . . so far, so good.

I'm starting to change a lot of my thinking concerning the Vietnamese. I need to have a lot more patience in dealing with cultural differences. In fact, I believe "patience" may be the number one virtue required to accomplish anything here. My counterpart exemplifies a majority of the officer class that I have observed. For instance, he is conceited, which appears to be a normal trait over here. He spends a lot of time looking at his own pictures, keeps himself very well groomed, and tries to impress any women we see in the villages. At the same time though, he seems to be well grounded in tactics, is not a risk taker, and is concerned about his troops . . . as long as it does not interfere with his own personal comfort.

This afternoon Mạnh, Chiến, and I drove into Bồng Sơn for some laundry and tailoring. On the way back, we ran into a firefight near one of the highway bridges. I radioed for help from battalion to reinforce the squad (about a dozen) of Regional Force (local militia) Vietnamese that were under fire. Receiving no response, I then called for Army helo gunships. By then we had one soldier shot three times in the leg, so I also called for a medevac. The VC were firing from about 100 yards away but withdrew as I approached. By the time the helos arrived, the VC were gone, and I called the medevac to land. I asked Mạnh to grab a smoke grenade and throw it in an open field to show wind direction to the pilot. It looked like white smoke and was drifting away from me as I cleared the pilot for landing. Unfortunately, it turned out to be tear gas, and I almost caused an accident as the tear gas enveloped the helo cockpit. Now there was a lesson learned! I'll check the smoke grenades myself from now on. And I'm sure the Army Warrant Officer pilot had a story to tell that evening about some crazy Marine!

About that same time, our 1st Company Commander came running up the road, almost 100 yards ahead of his Marines. He had just been notified by battalion and was coming to my rescue! He is one of the good ones! Later I found out that my assistant, the Gunny, had tried for 20 minutes to get the Battalion Commander to react to my request. But since it was only a local militia unit in trouble, there was little interest in responding.

Needless to say, this advisor role is a little different than being up north with US Marines and is going to be a real challenge. But I look forward to it and still believe it is the best solution to winning this war. During most nights there are no other Americans closer than a mile or so to me. You can see why I never let my radio get very far away and sleep with it at night!

9 JAN 68

I went over to TF A yesterday and talked with Maj Budd about how I felt and offered some recommendations. It seems that TF also has had some of the same concerns about my counterpart since he took command about two months ago. The battalion accident rate has gone up, and there are too many civilians wandering around our camp, especially women. I think my comments were taken to heart because Captain Vuong came over this morning and invited me to go to breakfast with him in Bồng Sơn. That was a first! Then this afternoon he came over to visit and told me what each of our companies was planning for tomorrow. That too was a first!

Just heard that Gene's 6th Battalion will arrive soon to relieve

Tom's 3rd Battalion. That should be fun to watch. Still not sure when the 4th Battalion will be relieved.

Our battalion Intelligence Officer has his wife visiting him for a while, and she invited me over to their hooch this evening for some bean soup and fish. It was delicious. I'm still amazed at how we can sit around a fried fish and pick it clean to the bone using only our chopsticks. I can almost keep up with them now. Not sure how this young wife is able to cope with this gypsy level camp. She appears to be in her early twenties, is well educated, speaks good English, and is well-mannered. She apparently came for a two-day visit and has been stuck here for about a month. There must be more to the story? She is the only officer's wife in our camp.

10 JAN 68

My counterpart invited me over to his bunker tonight for coffee and to listen to his new battery-powered phonograph. The change in our relationship is amazing since my trip to TF A! One thing that seems to have him completely baffled is the fact that I drink little or no alcohol, and I don't smoke. He wondered if that had anything to do with me not being tired on our last operation in the hills while he said he was very tired? I think we're making progress.

I invited Capt Vuong to TF A this afternoon for the 3rd Battalion going-away party. The TF Hq advisors had cooked hamburgers and steaks. Don't know where they came from, don't want to know! But my counterpart, being from North Vietnam, loved the meat.

Later, we made a helicopter reconnaissance of another objective area for a new operation on the 14th. The whole TF A will be going. I'm hoping it will be better than our last one.

Another highway culvert was just blown up by the VC. They never quit!

11 JAN 68

I received some instant breakfast packages in the mail and enjoyed one before the rats found them last night. Hope it makes them sick!

Tom passed by this morning with the 3rd Battalion, on the way to the Bồng Sơn airfield. Maj Budd was called back to Sài gòn with him. Gene arrived this afternoon with the 6th Battalion. I went down to TF A to welcome him and then he came back to my place to visit for a while. Isn't it a crazy war when I can visit with two friends halfway around the world who were my neighbors back in Woodbridge, VA?

I heard back from LtCol Leftwich. He and MGen Platt (the Commanding Officer of TBS when I served there) are both going to the funeral for LtCol Hatch.

13 JAN 68

VC were seen near our northernmost bridge, close to where I had my little smoke encounter the other day. They blew up a culvert south of there and demolished a big section of the highway. The Regional Forces ran away, and we couldn't get there in time, so the VC disappeared into the countryside.

Apparently, there is a lot of talk at TF about the shortcomings of my counterpart. I guess I didn't help any with my earlier visit and comments. But I do think that we are making progress as a team. I'm hoping that this next operation will give me a better chance to evaluate where we are. The previous battalion commander is back at Quantico attending AWS. He won't return until after I'm gone. It sounds like he was well-liked and respected. That might be part of the problem. I think we just need some more time to settle down.

It wouldn't be much longer before the two of us would be fighting for our lives in Sài gòn trying to keep the battalion from being overrun.

The Gunny has not been well lately. I think it is because he is very picky with his food and won't eat anything with soy sauce in it nor drink any of the soups they make. We don't have any C-rations, so we need to eat whatever they fix to keep our strength. He is a good Marine, but I don't think he is going to make it in the field with the Vietnamese.

There was a beautiful sunset this evening. Don't ever think I'm not enjoying myself. It just takes extra effort sometimes!

14 JAN 68

We had another briefing today, and it looks like we will start our next operation tomorrow morning. This time we will be in the valley and Gene's 6th Battalion will be up in the hills. We were also told that we will leave here on the 19th and return to our base camp in Vũng Tàu. I'm anxious to see it since it is supposed to be a beautiful seaside resort town.

It has started to rain again. Fun way to start the op in the morning.

15 JAN 68—*written from the 4th Battalion, VNMC CP somewhere in the valley near Bồng Sơn*

We are on the operation. I'm sitting in a vacated home that used to be beautiful. It's not very big by our standards, and it has a swept dirt floor, but the walls are paneled, it has big wooden ceiling beams, and it has a concrete patio in the rear. The roof is thatched and needs repair. Capt Vuong and I are sleeping on the floor in the main room, where there is a standard family altar, a small table, and some chairs. There is also a bedroom, cooking room, and some small storage nooks. An old woman with small children still lives here. There are no men around because this is VC country. They either join or they are killed! We killed three VC earlier, captured three more and picked up two M-16's and one carbine. I just had the prisoners flown out by helo for questioning. Gene has been watching from the hilltop and wishing he were down here. No action up there. I could have told him that based on our last op.

16 JAN 68

Things were slower today. We are back in the same house as before after a lot of walking. We picked up two more VC suspects, both female, but that was it for the day. Gene's battalion saw one VC but couldn't catch him! I enjoy being able to talk to Gene each night over the radio and compare notes.

17 JAN 68

I woke up about 4 am and couldn't sleep. Wandering around I found the Battalion Executive Officer, an old former enlisted Marine, now a captain with 27 years of experience going back to the French Legionnaires. He was sitting by a small lit candle, so I joined him. We talked and drank coffee and tea until daylight. Then my cowboy brought over a heated French roll with sausage. Wow! It was good!

I found out later that this old Marine had been the commander of the company that stormed the palace in Sài gòn during the last coup.

Our CP group is waking up now, and there are little campfires everywhere. Is this what it might have looked like during our own Civil War? There are little black pots of steaming rice perched above the flickering flames (probably not much rice during our Civil War). Here come the kids now. My Gunny loves the kids, and they seem to love him. He plays with them anytime we're not on the move. I have candy for them and give them some of my food.

It won't make any difference. Their daddies are VC, and after we leave, they will return. I hope we don't find them. Isn't there some way we could all sit down together and figure this out? It is beginning to rain and will be messy heading home.

The State of the Union message will be broadcast tomorrow over the Armed Forces network. I wonder if we will learn anything from it? I doubt it.

19 JAN 68

I think I'm actually gaining weight. My uniforms still feel loose, but I feel heavy. Must be the rice. I'm doing exercises every morning that we're not on an operation.

Gene's assistant, 1st Lt Wes Fox, was medevaced two nights ago with suspected hepatitis, but later the doctor said he was just dehydrated. Interesting to note that Wes is very picky and reluctant to eat any of the Vietnamese food.

Wes would later be transferred up north to the US Marines

and would be awarded the Medal of Honor for heroic actions as a Company Commander.

My Gunny made a deal for some steaks yesterday at the Army base in Bồng Sơn. They are for our going-away party this afternoon. Apparently, Maj Budd and the TF crew came along later and tried to talk him out of them to no avail. When they later complained back at TF, Gene told them to eat more Vietnamese food! That didn't go over so well, but they are all invited here later to share the steaks at our party. Hope that helps!

20 JAN 68

This afternoon, with the Gunny's help, we threw our going-away party. It was a big success. The Vietnamese really enjoyed it. Gene and I took turns cooking steaks, 40 of them! Yes, the Gunny is phenomenal and has been feeling much better since he developed his Army connection for chow.

We are packed up and ready to head for Vũng Tàu tomorrow. I'm excited and can't say I'm sorry to leave Bồng Sơn, but feel fortunate that I've been able to serve in very different places in such a short time.

I would end up serving and fighting in all four Corps zones before the end of the year.

21 JAN 68

I'm back in the bunker again. What an exasperating day in the pouring-down rain! We started at 5 am and moved 701 people to LZ English, north of Bồng Sơn, for our flight to Vũng Tàu. No one told us the move had been canceled last night. It took me an hour to confirm this. I was livid! Who needs TF if they can't coordinate a simple move like this? I went straight back to TF and respectfully addressed Maj Budd. I did not lose my temper, but it was close. I recommended an entirely new system of checking on plane schedules. How hard can that be? I'm not leaving here with 700 Marines and their equipment tomorrow until TF A can confirm the flight!

Enough complaining for now (*there would be much more later*). My counterpart came by to talk this evening, and we continue to make progress . . . patience, patience, patience. In the middle of the move this morning he headed back to his favorite haunt in Bồng Sơn, and I couldn't get anyone to move without his order. I know I can do this, but it won't be easy.

4

Finally made it to Vũng Tàu. It is great! The trip down here went smoothly for a change after some good coordination by TF A. Maj Budd accepted all of my recommendations. I guess it pays to sound off every now and then, when you think you're right. At least it did this time!

I am in a small but nice hotel room with a balcony and a hot water shower! It's called the Army/Navy (A/N) Hotel. I think all of the local US officer advisors live here full time, including my roommate. It is a short walk to the beach. The town is very pretty and much cleaner than Sài gòn . . . and much safer, too. This evening the Gunny and I walked around town for a while until our Marines found us, and then they wined and dined us until 10 pm. I'm stuffed! And we've been invited out tomorrow as well. Being able to speak a little Vietnamese and having our Marines watch out for us wherever we go is really great. I finally feel like I can relax for a while. There are a lot of Americans here, most of whom only speak English. I can joke behind their backs with the local Vietnamese, who love it. I talked with the woman who cleans our room for half an hour today. I'm so thankful for the MATA course and the language classes.

Tonight, I'll sleep in a bed with clean sheets after taking a hot shower and finally shampooing my hair . . . shades of my first night in Sài gòn after two months up in Đà nẵng. Tomorrow I'll probably walk down the beach. This place is nice enough to want to come back and visit after the war.

But I never have.

23 JAN 68

It is really hard to believe that there is a war going on around us! The usual signs of war are missing . . . no barbed wire, no demolished buildings, no people living in filth . . . so different than everywhere else I've been since arriving in-country. I almost feel like I'm on vacation . . . almost! Even my attitude has improved from my days at Bồng Sơn.

The Gunny and I drove around town in my Jeep today and we gave one of our battalion Marines a ride. He then took us to lunch. We were served noodle soup with pork, lime juice, hot peppers, mint leaves, and more. Then they brought us a cold drink that tasted like a coffee milkshake. It was all delicious!

Vũng Tàu is about a seven- or eight-block square with arteries extending along the seashore, rivershore, and back to the airstrip. The town faces the river. There is an open plaza in the middle with a huge roof, similar to our covered shopping malls back home. Another 4th Battalion Marine took us to dinner here, and it was even better than lunch. There were no other US troops in sight. We used chopsticks and spoke Vietnamese. The local people seemed to enjoy our company, and I enjoyed trying to converse with them. Before long, the manager was sending us extra meat and salad. Then he sent us glasses of bác sĩ đề, a Vietnamese whiskey. At this point, he appeared, sat down with us, and started drinking the whiskey. More food kept appearing as he talked to us only in Vietnamese. He spoke no English, but it was clear that he appreciated us and said that he did not like Vietnamese officers or VC! Not sure if that was for our benefit or not? But we finally excused ourselves and tried to pay for our meal. The manager would not hear of it, so we left a nice tip.

On the way back to the hotel we stopped at a coffee shop and had "coffee sua" . . . hot coffee poured over several spoonfuls of Eagle Brand. It is very good. Once again, we started talking in Vietnamese, and once again, the local people became very friendly. It seems so easy to get along with the local people if one just tries. However, other than the USO down the street, and the club at our hotel, I've not seen any other US military at any indigenous eating establishment. When I asked my US Army roommate, who is one of the advisors to the Vietnamese Military Police School located here about that, he said that he doesn't like the local food and doesn't care that much for the Vietnamese. How can he possibly be an effective advisor with that kind of attitude? If pervasive, that certainly would explain the lack of any other US military presence in town at local eating places.

Here is another tidbit that bothers me just a little! I found out that my roommate is drawing combat pay like all of us in-country, but unlike most of us, he is also being paid a Cost-of-Living Allowance to cover his hotel room and other hardship expenses! Hard to believe when compared to the way most of us have been living day-to-day. It seems like the US is encouraging these advisors to live more comfortably and apart from those we are here to help by paying them extra. I believe this same attitude helped lead to the downfall of the French.

My early observation is that the advisor program could and should be the key to victory. But that can never happen without a change in overall US attitude toward the Vietnamese. I noticed this same attitude among some of the US Marines up north, and believe that if it continues, we will have a much harder time winning this war.

I believe that only when the South Vietnamese themselves are willing and capable of overcoming the NVA and VC, will there be a chance to resolve this conflict. And only when the South Vietnamese can trust us will that begin to happen . . . and it needs to start at the top. One can only pray for a change in attitude and policy.

24 JAN 68—*written from Sài gòn*

The Gunny and I are back in Sài gòn. We will return as soon as I can sort out my pay record, which finally arrived from up north. The flight from Vũng Tàu was not uneventful. Although we showed up at 6 am and were in the air by 6:10, the cockpit filled with smoke at 6:15. I quickly rolled down my sleeves for fire protection as we heard two loud bangs! The pilot turned back to the field immediately and we landed successfully. Never did find out what went wrong. By

7:30, we were airborne again in a different plane, and we landed 35 minutes later in Sài gòn. And then our ground transportation got lost and it took another hour-and-a-half to pick us up.

Just heard that Bill U'ren was badly wounded (*he would lose his leg*) not far from where we ran some of our operations around Đà nẵng. I met one of the Marines who briefs Gen Westmoreland and he brought me up to speed on the action in I Corps. The NVA are really pounding Khe Sanh, where Charlie and the 26th Marines are dug in along the Demilitarized Zone (DMZ). I'm concerned about Charlie and the others we know up there. Incidentally, my new assistant advisor will be 1st Lt Bill Fite, who just returned from leave after extending for another year. He has been with the 26th Marines up on the DMZ. Hope to see him in a few days. I was one of his instructors at TBS. No surprise there.

I have been lucky so far in avoiding any heavy fighting and almost feel guilty, based on what's happening up north right now.

That was about to change big time!

26 JAN 68—*written from Vũng Tàu*

We are back in Vũng Tàu. It's good to be "home." I like it so much better down here. The weather is perfect. The people are great. It's not crowded. I can walk from my room to the USO and around town. I have my own Jeep if I want to drive to the beach or anywhere else.

The Gunny and I just walked over to the market to have some Vietnamese chow. He had invited the American woman who runs the USO to join us, but when she saw the Vietnamese food, she left!

28 JAN 68

Everyone is getting ready for Tết (the Vietnamese new year celebration) on 31 Jan. There have been non-stop battalion parties for the last two days, and since everyone is on holiday leave, I guess I am too, although we have been put on alert as one of the National Reserve Battalions.

. . . and the phone call would soon come!

I walked into town and had another wonderful lunch at the same place the manager had befriended us earlier. It cost all of 40 cents . . . and no other US military were in sight!

I moved out of the A/N Hotel, which is the BOQ and Officers Club. The Vietnamese call it the Palace Hotel . . . very fitting. The other advisors in town have created a small piece of the US there, surrounded by a fence and made it off-limits to the Vietnamese and all US enlisted personnel. From what I've read, this is exactly what the French did when they were here. I've moved into a small hotel, which is certainly adequate for me. The Vietnamese woman who cleans my room and washes my clothes every day brought me a small banana and French bread for breakfast this morning. I always try to talk with her each day in her language. I know she appreciates it, and it also helps my proficiency.

This afternoon I helped pass out CARE packages to our battalion enlisted Marine families. From what I've seen they can certainly use the goodies. Later my counterpart invited me to join him and a few other Vietnamese officers to "go out on the town!" He has warmed up to me considerably since our Bồng Son experience. I wonder if I've misjudged him?

The only church I've found close by has been Catholic, but I'm still looking for a Protestant one. I miss that part of Sunday each week.

29 JAN 68

Today is the eve before Tết begins, which will last about two days. Most of the US military have been restricted from going anywhere in town other than the A/N hotel. I still wander around freely in my tiger suit and talk to the locals as I've done since arriving. The Military Police know me by now and leave me alone since I'm almost always with the Vietnamese. The USO was empty this evening when I went in to write letters, as I've done before. I talked with the American who runs it and the Vietnamese girls who work there. They brought me ice cream and some cookies they had just baked. The director has a Peace Corps background and has set up clubs all over the country. He has been over here for more than a year and also speaks Vietnamese . . . an interesting guy.

This morning the battalion hosted a series of outdoor field events for the troops and their families. They blindfolded several of us and had us swing a stick at clay pots hanging by a wire. As the pots were broken, there were many surprises . . . cookies, water, sand, and live chickens and ducks! Yep, mine yielded a chicken, much to the enjoyment of all. I haven't laughed that hard in a long time. Barbecued crab was served with other delicacies later. Then the officers went to a small restaurant facing the beach . . . and we ate again as we watched the waves coming in.

30 JAN 68

There are more ceremonies and parties today. My counterpart asked me to present a Cross of Gallantry medal to one of our Marines today. It is the Vietnamese equivalent of our Bronze Star for bravery. I felt very honored. Afterward, I was invited along with our officers to Capt Vuong's home in town for a champagne dinner. He has a lovely wife, and his home is large by Vietnamese standards. The food was delicious and special for Tết. I took small envelopes with money for their two children, which I had been told was the custom.

These last few days have made up for all my previous frustrations. This is truly a special celebration for the Vietnamese. A truce has been called between the North and South to honor Tết. Everyone is looking forward to more celebrations tomorrow.

My hotel roommate, the one who won't eat any local food, has been sick for two days. I took him to the hospital, and he was diagnosed with an intestinal infection! Poor guy can't understand it.

5

3 FEB 68—*written from the US Army 17th Field Hospital, Sài gòn*

We flew from Vũng Tàu to Sài gòn on the morning of the 31st and were in almost continuous contact with the enemy until now. We beat off two mass assaults and finally caused them to withdraw. I was wounded about 3 am yesterday, along with my cowboy and radio operator, during a mortar and rocket barrage. An exploding mortar round hit me in both arms and my left leg, but I'm in the hospital and the doctor has fixed me up. Nothing serious. Too much has happened too fast to try and write it all down right now . . . maybe later. It's not over yet. There is still fighting going on here and around the country. By the time you receive this letter, I hope to be healed and back with the battalion. I wouldn't let the Red Cross send a telegram because it would not have any details and I thought it might cause undue concern.

My world turned upside down at 5:30 am on 31 Jan. My driver banged on my hotel room door and told me that our battalion had been ordered to Sài gòn and that Capt Vuong and the 4th Battalion were on the way to the airfield. I quickly dressed, grabbed my gear and weapon, and jumped in the jeep. At the airfield, I was told that the NVA and VC had launched a coordinated attack throughout South Vietnam and that Australian C-130 transport aircraft were landing to take us to Sài gòn. As I began to coordinate the airlift, it struck me that I would be the only advisor with the battalion. Somehow, we managed to load 700 Marines with their machine guns, mortars, and a small amount of ammo. However, we couldn't land at the Tân Sơn Nhứt airport in Sài gòn until 9:30 due to heavy fog and ground fire. Happy Tết!

Once we landed, Capt Vuong and I were briefed by the senior Vietnamese and US Army advisor at the airport. I also found an Army friend from AWS that gave me a city map and a few radio frequencies for coordinating fire support. Then off we went by foot through town. Our main objective was an ARVN armor compound east of Tân Sơn Nhứt. We passed by numerous back-alley firefights between the ARVN soldiers and the VC but couldn't afford to stop. We also passed the US Embassy, which had been overrun during the night but had just been retaken by an ARVN force. There were still enemy bodies lying in the front of the embassy.

I would later end up in a hospital bed next to John Gardner, one of the US embassy employees who had been shot several times across his chest with an AK-47.

Finally, a couple of VC platoons, about 50 soldiers, surprised us with crossfire and stopped us about a mile-and-a-half from our objective. We started taking casualties right away, and I was frantically and unsuccessfully trying to reach any kind of air support over my radio. Just then, a couple of ARVN tanks and armored personnel carriers showed up. By now we had civilians intermingling between our troops and the VC, and I had two NBC reporters and a few others following me. Since there was no way to move forward without causing many civilian casualties, we pulled back and went around. As far as I could determine, we were the only VNMC battalion committed at this time and I was still without an assistant advisor.

As we continued down city streets toward our objective, the local people offered us soft drinks, water, watermelon, etc., which was accepted gratefully. There had been no time to eat since leaving Vũng Tàu. By midafternoon we were again in contact, and this time it was heavier. I was not getting any cooperation from the Tân Sơn Nhứt folks, since they said they had other priorities at the time. So we continued to push forward with what we had and finally reached the compound. There were high observation towers around it, giving the enemy a distinct advantage. My initial assessment was that the towers would need to be neutralized and the main gate would need to be blown open for us to enter.

Before we began to plan our assault, the NVA let us know they were holding the ARVN LtCol in command of the compound and his family as hostages and would kill them if we attacked. My counterpart and I discussed it and decided to attack anyway. It was a hard but necessary decision. There was no way to know at the time if the NVA were bluffing or if the hostages were still alive.

By now I had coordinated with a couple of US Army helicopter gunships to support us as we probed the compound. They were very helpful in neutralizing the towers while our mortars and supporting artillery softened the enemy. We called a tank forward and had it knock down the main gate, and we rushed in behind it. Things were initially chaotic, but we had the initiative, and the NVA fell back as we penetrated the compound. However, as darkness came over us and the helo gunships needed to refuel and rearm, we had to pull out, regroup, and resupply. We were almost out of ammo! We had counted over 100 enemy KIA and 35 captured weapons. Our own losses were small in comparison.

Unfortunately and regrettably, we found the LtCol and his family were all dead. They had been shot and set on fire behind one of the barracks. These images of war never leave you and are cause for reflection for years to come. I can only hope that God can forgive us for the things that we do in war.

As we pulled back into nearby neighborhoods for protection, US helo gunships and Vietnamese bombers mistook us for the bad guys and started firing at us. It took extreme effort to get them to stop shooting into us. Afterward, I located a three-way intersection that I thought might work for a helo resupply of ammo. There were houses and power lines close by, but I was sure a skilled pilot could land there . . . and we desperately needed the ammo for our attack tomorrow.

My counterpart and I coordinated with the Vietnamese Air Force, which sent a helicopter loaded with ammo for our resupply. It arrived at 2 am, and we lit the area with a couple of jeep headlamps. It was tight, but the pilot did a nice job. We were supposed to receive a second helo resupply, but we never saw the pilot again! We would have to go with what we had. The rest of the night was spent rationing out the ammo. By now I had developed a real set of stomach cramps that would stay with me until I reached the hospital the following evening.

At first light on 1 Feb, Maj Bill McKinstry arrived in Sài gòn from down south with all available advisors from TF B. He brought the MAU administrative officer, Capt John Hainsworth, to be my assistant, and the 1st Battalion, VNMC with Capt Jerry Simpson to back us up. Both Maj McKinstry and Jerry were friends from Quantico. It was really good to see them! I also now had US air support and ARVN tanks standing by to support our assault. We would need them both since I was sure the NVA had strengthened their defenses during the night.

Our assault went well, and we were able to penetrate the NVA defenses and push them out of the compound once again. Later in the afternoon, the 1st Battalion passed through us and set up to our left front, still inside the compound, which covered most of a city block. They were hit immediately by a sizable force, but Jerry did a good job calling in air support and coordinating artillery fire, which broke up the enemy attack. We then pulled up on the 1st Battalion right flank. Enemy contact was now sporadic. Our losses were still very light, but we had another 50 NVA KIA and picked up 40 more weapons.

We consolidated our position and tended to our wounded and dead. We had also captured two NVA officers alive and processed them back to higher Hq.

The next day I was told the Sài gòn Police Chief, BGen Loan, executed one of those officers publicly and in view of a photographer. The event would make the cover of Newsweek magazine and become one of the most widely circulated pictures of the war. What was not published at the time was that the LtCol, who had been murdered along with his family by the NVA during our assault, had been a personal friend of Gen Loan.

As darkness fell, we tightened up our security in the compound, and I lay down on the porch of one of the buildings and fell asleep. I had been up for almost two days.

At 3 am on 3 Feb, my world came apart again, but this time with deafening explosions! I rose up to grab my radio as two more *rounds exploded close by. The concussion picked me up and bounced me against the side of the building. I didn't feel any pain at the time but knew I had been hit. I checked on John, who had been nicked in the finger but was okay.*

My cowboy and radioman had been hit and were hard down. I steadied myself, located my radio, which fortunately had not been hit, and started to look for my counterpart, who was behind me flat on the ground up against some steps. He was okay.

We determined that a counterattack was underway with incoming mortar and rocket fire. In fact, by then the NVA were coming over the back wall of the compound! Our young Marines were holding their own, but I knew we needed additional support quickly if we were going to survive the night!

The 1st Battalion was also under attack, and Jerry and I took turns calling in air strikes and artillery rounds. We were calling for anybody that would answer and fire for us. Thank goodness for illumination rounds. It gave us the ability to turn darkness into daylight and to be able to see where to fire against the enemy. It also allowed the aircraft to see what we were marking and asking them to shoot and bomb.

At one point the NVA broke through the wall and were inside the compound. Fortunately, I was coordinating with a young Army advisor with the ARVN Artillery compound next to us, and he lowered the barrels of his 105mm howitzers and fired directly down the length of the wall. That gave us time to clean up those few NVA that had penetrated our front line. I've never waited so long nor ever been happier to see dawn arrive! With daylight, I could coordinate with an airborne USAF forward air controller (FAC) to direct the Vietnamese bombers to drop 500-pound bombs and napalm within 50 yards of our front lines. I sent John forward with our lead company to mark our position with colored smoke for the pilots to see . . . and then we all got down low and prayed. It worked, and at about 8:55, what was left of the NVA battalion appeared to break contact and retreat. However, as we rose up and took a long breath, they brought up a reserve unit and resumed the attack!

This time the FAC linked us up with a USAF C-130 aircraft that had a 105mm howitzer firing out of its side door. We marked our front lines again and asked him to fire at anything that moved on the other side. By noon, things had settled down, and there was no sign of enemy movement. We sent one company forward to search the battlefield and found another 75 enemy KIA. We only had nine KIA, but more than 100 wounded.

It was a hard-fought battle by both sides, and I was proud of our Vietnamese Marines. They had held their ground when it counted. We had beaten the NVA, but it had not been easy. Since arriving in Sài gòn, we had lost close to 200 killed or wounded. Although we were not able to get an accurate count of enemy casualties since they dragged many of them away, our best estimate from weapons left and blood trails was that they also lost around 200 soldiers.

As we licked our wounds and reset our defensive posture, just in case there was going to be a replay of last night, we began to evacuate our dead and wounded. John had bandaged up my worst arm soon after I was hit and then helped take care of many of the wounded Vietnamese. The Battalion bác sĩ (doctor) had checked me over, stopped all the bleeding, and stuck me with a needle full of something, but it was evident that I needed some more work done. I had one fragment that had gone through my left bicep and was sticking out the other side.

Capt Vuong apparently had reported through his radio channels that I had been wounded and would need to be evacuated. Jerry also had called for a replacement. He had been sick for several weeks, and it had finally sapped away his strength. About 6 pm, replacements for Jerry and me showed up in a jeep. My relief was Capt Brad Bagley. I had met him back in Đà nẵng when we both checked in to the 1st Marine Division. He was a Public Information Officer (PIO). We were short on advisors. I hoped that they could fix me up quickly so I could return.

Jerry and I got into the jeep and were escorted by an armed guard back to the MAU and then to the hospital. I'm afraid my appearance was somewhat lacking for a squared-away Marine. I had four days *growth of beard, and my green utilities were now brown with dirt, dried blood and sweat. I was filthy, smelly, and tired, and I hurt a little bit. LtCol Rodney, the assistant Senior Marine Advisor, escorted me to the hospital and stayed with me while a doctor and Army medics cut off my jacket and trousers, completed the X-rays, and began the surgery. I had shell fragments in my left thigh, left forearm, and both biceps, and a sliver in my nose right between my eyes. Fortunately, nothing vital had been hit, but they were not able to reach all the fragments in my arms without doing unnecessary damage. They left all the incisions open for a few days to drain and made sure I didn't become infected. Then they sewed me up with stainless steel wire, leaving souvenirs in both arms, which I still carry to this day. I was a little embarrassed being in the hospital with so many others who were much more seriously wounded since I felt pretty good. In the bed next to me was John Gardner, who was in the US Embassy when it was overrun. He had been shot five times across the chest by a VC with an AK-47 assault rifle and was in bad shape. He made it, though. I had seen enough combat to last me for a while, but there would be more to come!*

4 FEB 68

There is still some fighting going on here in Sài gòn, but mostly on the outskirts. Other than a few advisors getting sick, I'm the only one that was wounded so far. Based on what I've heard, we were very lucky. I feel like going back to the battalion, but the doctor says I need to wait a few more days. Several of the advisors, who are now in town have stopped by to see me and bring mail. I really appreciate them.

1st Lt Bill Fite, my new assistant, has arrived and is with our battalion. I don't have any idea how long they will remain in this area, but I'm hoping to join them before they take off somewhere. What was left of the NVA units has retreated into the countryside and is probably headed for Laos and Cambodia to rebuild their units. The VC have faded into the city and we will probably never find them unless the local people turn them in.

6 FEB 68

All the seriously wounded here in the hospital have been transferred back to the states. Half the beds are now empty, and of those that are left, half of them are not wounded, just sick. The doctor just said he will sew me up tomorrow and I can return to the battalion.

Another interesting tidbit . . . yesterday two NFL players from the New York Giants stopped in to "cheer us up!" There is still some occasional sniper fire that whistles by every now and then . . . and with all the commotion we had a few days ago, they seemed a little bit unsure of themselves and didn't stay long! They left a bunch of stuff that I'll send home for the kids when I get the chance.

7 FEB 68

The doctor sewed me up with stainless steel wire this morning and will discharge me tomorrow. I think one reason they kept me here so long is that they realized that I was going to be living with the battalion in the countryside, not in some hotel with running water! But I will be so glad to return to my other life. All six VNMC battalions are back in Sài gòn. No wonder things have slowed down and the NVA left!

I sat out on a small hospital balcony for a while today and the traffic is slowly starting to pick up. There is a curfew that only allows the people to be on the street from 8 am to 2 pm.

9 FEB 68

I found the 4th Battalion where I had left them, still in the Armor compound. They have been doing house-to-house checks for VC with no results and are moving into one of the nearby areas. The 1st Battalion has left and headed north. I'm guessing we may follow. There is still some fighting going on up there. Right now, I'm engulfed with all the reports and paperwork required to document our actions since arriving in Sài gòn.

10 FEB 68

We are still in Sài gòn. Don't know why we haven't been committed again. There was a battalion-size battle against the VC not far from here and I could only watch the airstrikes and artillery fire. Bill Fite is fitting into the battalion nicely. He is studying the language and trying to learn to speak it from scratch since he did not have a chance to go to MATA.

I'm sleeping in the living room of one of the vacated homes tonight with a mosquito net hung over me. The weather is warm and damp, and the mosquitoes are hungry!

11 FEB 68

Still here. We had a light probe by some VC last night. I called in helo gunships and broke it up within a half hour. Not sure how many of them we hurt, but we had two wounded. It's not good for us to just sit here in the city and be targets. We need to get out of here.

12 FEB 68

Still here. Still writing reports. John Hainsworth had the sliver in his finger, suffered during our battle for the compound, removed today at the MAU by another advisor with a set of tweezers! Everyone cheered!

The only good part of being here right now is being able to receive mail every day. That has been a real morale boost and makes up for all the rest.

6

15 FEB 68—*written from Phú Bài*

We finally were committed yesterday and flew up to Phú Bài, just south of Huế in I Corps. We will be going into the walled part of Huế (the Citadel) as soon as I can talk the US Marines here into giving us transportation up to the Perfume River. Our Senior Advisor, Col Michael, flew up with us and we talked with the Marine general in charge several times today, trying to coordinate our move. It looks like they will move us in the morning. Our 1st and 5th VNMC Battalions are already in the Citadel and are in contact, along with some ARVN units and the US Marine 2nd Battalion, 5th Marines. The Perfume River divides the town in half from west to east and then from south to north. There were several bridges crossing the river, but they have all been blown up by the NVA, who still occupy the southern part of the Citadel. The Citadel is across the river to the north and west. We will need to use boats once we arrive at the river in order to get across and land further up the Perfume River to the north. Our mission along with the other units inside the Citadel is to retake it from the NVA! Sound familiar?

Huế, the ancient imperial capital city of Vietnam, was about 62 miles south of the DMZ. It had a population of nearly 140,000, making it the third largest city in South Vietnam, behind Sài gòn and Đà nẵng. The Citadel or Imperial City was the walled portion of Huế sitting on the north bank of the Perfume River and surrounded by a moat. The four walls were built with stone, and each was about a mile and a half long.

I've just heard that another friend from TBS, Maj Walt Murphy, was killed after crossing the main bridge before it was blown up.

Two other good friends from TBS and AWS are with Marine units already in contact with the NVA in Hué.

16 FEB 68—*written from inside the Hué Citadel*

The US Marines drove us up to the river in their trucks this morning. Once there, I was able to coordinate with Maj Bob Kurlick, another friend from Quantico, who was in charge of scheduling the boat traffic. He loaded our battalion plus a few other hitchhikers on several boats. A female French reporter rode with us and followed us into the Citadel. I heard later that she was killed while with the US Marines.

The boats headed north up the Perfume River and then approached from the east. We offloaded and entered into the Citadel through the most northern entrance. The NVA have been pushed back into the southern part where an old castle sits. We dug in next to the northern half of the west wall. The wall is massive . . . two stories high and wide enough on top for a two-lane road. It is square-shaped, surrounded by a moat, with each side being about a mile-and-a-half long. The gateway entrances into the Citadel are more like tunnels. Some of the NVA in front of us have dug into the wall for protection and have the advantage of elevation. The rest are barricaded in residential neighborhoods and are dug in at each intersection, able to provide intersecting fires up and down the streets. It will be hard to advance without supporting fires from both artillery and air. We have already had one Marine wounded as we were settling in.

17 FEB 68

The weather is not good. It rains off and on day and night. I managed to call in one close air support mission today, but the pilot aborted due to enemy ground fire. Helo gunships were ready to support our assault, but the mission was denied by TF A because they wanted more artillery preparation fires. I had already called in 105mm, 8", and 155mm artillery and we were ready to go. Later Bill Fite, with the help of covering fire from one helo gunship, rescued one of our Marines, who was wounded trying to charge a bunker on top of the wall. Sadly, the young Marine died. We have now suffered 1 KIA and 12 more wounded since we arrived in Hué. It was a frustrating day!

18 FEB 68

Today TF A check-fired (stopped firing) almost every 8" mission I called. Even Capt Vuong was getting frustrated, although he rarely leaves his foxhole. I am unable to get any priority of fires for our battalion, and there is a decided lack of fire support coordination from above. I headed back to TF Hq, explained our frustration, and requested help. I suspect there might be a breakdown between counterparts at their level. Shades of Bồng Sơn!

19 FEB 68

This afternoon we moved south from the NW corner and relieved the 5th Battalion, who had reached the SW wall. They had suffered many casualties yesterday from heavy mortar attacks. I am in a foxhole in the back yard of a small home. I have a tin cover to divert most of the rain. It has been raining nonstop for the last two days. I haven't been able to coordinate any air support due to the weather. However, with renewed TF support, I've been able to call several artillery missions today, but they have not been effective in dislodging the enemy. The enemy is too well dug in and highly disciplined. I can only hope that we can coordinate enough artillery fire to force the enemy to keep their heads down long enough for us to attack through them. We continue to receive sporadic sniper, 82mm mortar, and B40 rocket fire.

The challenge was that fighting block by block in a residential section and trying to call in an area weapon like artillery or air support on the enemy put our own Marines at risk since we were just across the street from the bad guys.

We cannot return mortar fire because we have no 60mm mortars with us at the company level. We can only carry so much weight and chose 57mm recoilless rifles (RR) instead for their bunker-penetrating power in city fighting.

However, we found the 57mm RR was not enough. We needed the US Marine 106 RR, which fired a much larger round.

We do have one 81mm mortar with us, which will probably never be fired unless we are about to be overrun. We really need it right now, but conflicting reports on limited ammo make it nearly impossible to request. There is mounting political pressure from higher Hq for us to move forward, but without a break in the weather and better fire-support coordination that I can count on, it will take a lot of individual and small-unit sacrifice to uproot this enemy. We did have two 76mm ARVN tanks show up today, but they will be of limited use in this close in city fighting.

The Citadel was a beautiful place. Many of the homes had modern plumbing fixtures and ornate furnishings. Most of the homes to the NW are still intact, but there are very few to the SW that are not heavily damaged. All are looted as soon as we arrive. The local inhabitants have either been killed or have left the area long before we arrive. Yesterday, a few started to return to the northern sections for the first time since Tết began. The battalion fed them rice, and they seemed grateful.

One of the more interesting sidelights to this long battle is the enemy radio frequency that we monitor. We are able to find out how much damage we are doing and the casualties we are inflicting. Of course, they are monitoring us as well, and it is interesting to see how they react to our transmissions.

When I was briefed earlier in Phú Bài for this operation, I wondered at the time why we had not surrounded and sealed off the Citadel before we went inside. Without resupply, surely the NVA could not last very long.

We had taught this at TBS as a basic infantry tactic. I found out much later that the initial deployment of forces into Huế was made without good intelligence and led to many unnecessary casualties.

But now that we are inside, we will continue to monitor the enemy's radio frequency and find out when they are evacuating their wounded from the castle, and when they are receiving supplies through the western entrance to our right front (the Hữu Gate), which they still control. I've called in artillery on and around the entrance tunnel they are using, but the wall is too thick to penetrate. I've requested that higher Hq send another unit around from outside the wall to seal off that gate, and I'm told that a US Army unit is on the way, but it will take time for them to arrive. How much time will probably determine how much longer this battle will last!

How right I was! The Army unit was delayed and suffered heavy losses when they ran into the NVA Command HQ to the north, which was heavily defended. But our battle did end as they finally arrived!

Although I have experienced maximum frustration during the last few days, I've also experienced the ultimate in trying to advise my counterpart. He began asking for my tactical advice on almost everything several days ago. He has accepted much of it and rejected very little. Our biggest point of contention has been his refusal to assault with no air support available. He does not trust the artillery support, and it has been unreliable at times, but to sit here and take casualties from incoming enemy mortars and rockets is not a good trade-off! Having been wounded once already, I'm not in favor of just sitting and waiting. I don't think he has left his foxhole since he climbed into it. It didn't help matters any this morning when the 5th Battalion was calling in an artillery mission and one round fell short on friendly troops! This is the longest sustained battle the VNMC has had to fight so far, and it is taking a toll. The battalion has been in almost continuous contact, except for the last few days in Sài gòn, since the 31st of January.

20 FEB 68

We were ordered to attack this morning and, for a while, were given priority of fires. I called in 8" and 155mm artillery, and we were able to advance until several errant rounds landed too close for comfort. That ended that! I waited all day on air support, but the weather did not cooperate. All in all, we moved about two blocks, knocked out one NVA command post, and picked up several machine guns and rifles. We tried using tear gas on the enemy today since we had gas masks with us, but they also had masks or covered their face with wet cloths. We will tune in to the enemy radios again tonight and see if we can figure out their casualties. Our losses continue to mount.

21 FEB 68

We have been here since 16 February and made very little progress. We tried to break through along the SW wall and got nowhere. The weather has not been good, negating our ability to use air support since our first day . . . and then it was only marginal. A major problem has been lack of direction. Orders from above have not been specific enough, leaving too much to the battalion commander's discretion. He, in turn, is placing too much reliance on air support, which of course, has not been available. All of our commanders are unsure of artillery support since they cannot depend on higher Hq to give them priority of fire when they need it.

As I've mentioned before, the TF Commander did not establish priority of fire support for the needy battalion during our first few days. In an earlier instance, our attack was halted when TF refused to allow air to support us, because they had decided to have artillery fire on the same target. As everything became confused, we lost our momentum with negative results.

Although individual Marines and company/platoon commanders seem willing to do whatever they are told, battalion commanders are reluctant to move without overwhelming fire support. I have not been able to provide that to date. TF has made a concerted effort to restrict the use of lower caliber Vietnamese 105mm artillery in favor of heavier caliber US 155mm and 8" artillery. Not sure if the reason has to do with the limited Vietnamese ammo supply or not, but the increased bursting radius of the heavier artillery makes it much more dangerous and harder to fire in close proximity to our troops. We set a precedent the other day by "creeping" a round of the heavier artillery toward our front lines, a few meters at a time, until we were firing within 300 meters. We had excellent results. But we have to have supporting fires closer than 300 meters to keep from taking excessive casualties. (*The NVA were dug into spider holes at every street intersection and along the wall.*)

22 FEB 68

Washington's Birthday started off about 5:45 am with several volleys of 122mm and 140mm rockets from the countryside into our positions. We took quite a few casualties. It was a scary feeling huddled in a foxhole covered with a tin roof, listening to the split-second shrill screams of the incoming rockets, wondering how close the next one would be. Fortunately, I was a little better protected than in Sài gòn, but one of them did hit our enlisted medical section and killed three of them. It hit on the other side of the garden wall next to me, and the baseplate from one rocket landed next to my foxhole (*I still have it today*). The rocket barrage was not totally unexpected since our radio discipline has been very poor. Last night, the entire operation was discussed over the radio, and I'm sure the NVA were listening. I will try to discuss with TF and see if they will set the example. This afternoon I coordinated with Marine F-4 aircraft to drop napalm and 500-pound bombs on top of the wall. That bought us a little more time to move forward again. It didn't stop the NVA from popping back out of their holes afterward, but I'm sure they at least had headaches!

This evening before dark, I made a run for TF to pick up new mail that had just arrived. Only a hot shower and a clean pair of socks could come close to producing such happiness!

23 FEB 68

It's about 4 pm, and I have just enjoyed a cup of cold rice and a warm can of sardines. This is the first time we've had a chance to eat since yesterday afternoon. We started our assault this morning with the promise from TF of priority artillery support, and received nothing! I was not able to provide any air support because it has rained all day. I really felt like I had let the battalion down. The Vietnamese are starting to feel like they cannot count on US support.

Meanwhile, the US Marines on the other side of the Citadel reached the southeast wall this morning. They raised a US flag. Later today, they were ordered to lower it and raise the South Vietnamese flag. Now the pressure is really on us to finish the job on the west side! Maybe now we will receive priority of US fire support. The 1st Battalion has been on our left flank during this attack and lost two armored personnel carriers today due to poor employment, which in turn was due, I believe, to lack of fire support from higher Hq.

24 FEB 68

This morning Col Michael showed up with two US Marines and their Ontos (a small low tank looking vehicle with six 106mm recoilless rifles attached) now that their fight was over. We used it to pinpoint enemy gun locations in the wall and blow them out. That allowed us to cross the last street and advance to the last block. The rest of the city is secured. We will finish it tonight!

What I had not realized at the time was that the NVA had started to withdraw during the night through the Hữu and Nha Đồ SW Gates that we had not yet been able to reach.

25 FEB 68

It's over! We attacked at 2 am and I'm huddled in a bunker up on the top of the southwest wall. It has been a whale of a fight! It took us five days to secure the last four blocks in the southwest corner. The US Army unit finally arrived from the north last night and sealed off the entrance being used for resupply by the enemy, but not before the NVA started withdrawing, and most escaped. They left soldiers chained to their machine guns inside houses, which caused us a few more casualties before it was over. Tragically, the two young Ontos Marines, who provided such great support for us, were killed on the way back to their unit by one of the NVA stay-behind machine gun crews.

This morning at 5 am, we cleared the last house that still had an active machine gun inside. Our Marines went through the roof to capture these last two soldiers. The prisoners, when questioned, told us that they had been led to believe, before they left North Vietnam, that they would be marching in victory parades when they arrived in Hué.

The NLF (National Liberation Front) in Hanoi had counted on the people of Hué to rise up and welcome the NVA forces and help overthrow the ARVN and US units. It did not happen.

We landed in Sài gòn with 701 Marines almost a month ago. We are down to 431 today, counting the replacements we picked up before flying up to Phú Bài. We had heavier casualties here than in Sài gòn. The NVA we faced inside the Citadel seemed smarter and tougher than those in Sài gòn. The entrenchments and bunkers they prepared were textbook. We all paid a heavy price for this win. Bill Fite's cowboy and radioman were wounded here, as were mine in the Sài gòn battle. Not sure why anyone else would want to work for either of us!

The local people are starting to enter the southwest section of town and start their long road to recovery. You can feel their sadness as they approach their homes and see a smile of gladness as they find some small item that is still intact. I haven't seen a home yet in this section that was not at least partially destroyed. This whole area is indescribable. So much of this damage and so many lives lost might have been mitigated, had we used another strategy to secure the Citadel.

On a different note, my wounds have healed, and I asked another advisor at TF Hq to pull out my wire stitches yesterday. I'm fine. No infections. I have no idea what happens next, but we are prepared to move when ordered.

I am dirty and wet and cold and hoping my gear catches up with me soon. I'll be so happy to bathe, even with cold water, and finally change clothes.

1967 DANANG

1967 BONG SON

1967 BONG SON

1967 BONG SON

1967 BONG SON

1968 TET, SAIGON

1968 TET, SAIGON

1968 TET, SAIGON

1968 TET, HUE CITADEL

1968 TET, HUE CITADEL

1968 CAN THO

7

This morning our battalion moved out of the Citadel to the east and on to an island in the Perfume River. We will clear it and then rest, I think. There are still some VC around, so we need to stay alert, but I think the worst is over. The NVA left a lot of almost new gear when they pulled out of the Citadel. I believe they must have been one of the North's top units. I've picked up a lot of their stuff which I will share with the other advisors. We passed by a few unburied NVA bodies as we moved out of the Citadel. There is rubble everywhere, burned-out and wrecked vehicles at most intersections, and deserted trenches and bunkers all over.

Before we left, Colonel Michael brought the Army general in charge of the Huế operation to our positions and I gave him a tour. He had been out before and we had discussed my problems of support, i.e. not having the outside entrances to the Citadel blocked, and delays in getting priority of fire support when we needed it to advance. Col Michael has been very helpful throughout and at one point called Gen Westmoreland. Things started to improve after that! I might add that our TF senior advisor left for R&R about the time we arrived in Huế. I guess that surprised me a little bit.

We're staying in a school building with all the windows broken, but the walls and roof are intact, so it is dry. It is still raining, and it's cold, but the MAU sent me two new uniforms to wear, so I clenched my teeth and cleaned up with COLD water! Not fun, but it was worth it.

28 FEB 68

Bill Fite and I drove back into the Citadel today and walked over our part of the battlefield and through the castle. They were using the castle as a hospital. It was quite depressing, and I couldn't wait to leave. The local people are working hard to rebuild their homes, in some cases one brick or stone at a time . . . and every member of the family is helping. Many of their homes are missing the roof and most of the walls. The damage we did to the city, especially to the old castle and wall, is horrible, but in the stress of combat, when lives are at stake, hard choices have to be made.

We had some vegetables with our rice today. Other than the rice, we have lived off of pork and one unfortunate dog since departing Sài gòn. I have appreciated the goodies that I've received from home when they can be delivered. However, when we move on foot, I am limited in how much I can carry. The less I carry with me, the faster and easier it is to keep moving. I have had to leave things in Vũng Tàu and Sài gòn until my Jeep can catch up with me. Sometimes it takes several days or even weeks for that to happen.

Another month is gone, with much to remember and much more for which to be grateful. I am still happy and content with my job. My only regret is that I have to be separated from my family so long in order to fulfill my responsibility to my country.

I believe it was harder by far for my family to be back home and not know in real time what we were involved in over here, except by reading about it in newspapers and hearing it on the six o'clock news. This past month especially was difficult since my letters, when I could write and when they could be mailed, were taking one to two weeks to reach home. I didn't help matters any when I chose to write Pat and my Mom from the hospital, after I was wounded, rather than let the Red Cross inform them . . . and my Mom's letter arrived first!

29 FEB 68—*Leap Year Day*

Today was spent writing reports . . . all day.

1 MAR 68

We are still here. Bill Fite and I walked around town again today. The sun is finally out and feels warm. Too bad we didn't have this weather during the battle. We could have finished it much sooner. At first, the canals and river look beautiful, until we look beyond and see the rubble, a burned-out tank, and more destruction. I feel good that we were able to liberate this city for the people who live here, and that they seem to appreciate it by smiling back at us. I just wish we could have done it with less devastation.

2 MAR 68

Still here. It has started to rain again. The good news is that my original radioman, Mạnh, returned today. He received a bad head wound in Sài gòn and is still about half-speed. I took a long nap today. It really felt good. I had not realized how tired I had become.

I just heard that Gen Westmoreland sent US Army Gen Abrams up here to be in charge of I Corps; the Marines have been in charge until now. Wonder what that is about? Sounds like politics to me.

Years later, my concerns over how we were fighting this war would be borne out by men far smarter than I. Gen Westmoreland's critics would say his emphasis on attrition numbers (body counts) rather than changing attitudes and having US units win rather than the South Vietnamese was a recipe for disaster. In addition, the US was providing the South Vietnamese units with our older, less capable equipment, which did not send a good message about our confidence in their capabilities. As a result, the NVA units we faced had newer and better equipment. At the same time, the US Marines in I Corps had started assigning Civic Action Platoons (CAP) to local villages to help them defend themselves. It was having some success before the US was pulled out of Vietnam. The CAP program, along with US advisors who lived with Vietnamese main line units and could teach their counterparts how best to use supporting arms, might well have been a recipe for success, had it been given a fair chance. Fast forward to the recent war . . . wars in the Middle East, where Gen Petraeus ordered a similar strategy for US forces.

3 MAR 68

Still here. Completed more paperwork today. Still more to go. No church to attend. Will read my prayer book instead. It has meant a lot to me.

My Mom had given me a small prayer book to carry before I left for Vietnam.

Now that the battle in the city against the NVA is over and has left so much rubble, trash, and destruction, it is time to reflect on what has happened, and what we might have learned. The NVA are tough, tenacious, disciplined, and professional fighters. Even with young teenagers in their ranks who had been told they would be marching in victory parades in the south, they were able to maintain their effectiveness while in heavy combat situations. What strange power Hanoi must have over these soldiers.

The situation we faced in Huế was even more intense than what we experienced in Sài gòn. With the massive wall encircling the Citadel, another aspect was added to an already complex task of fighting in a built-up area. We learned in Sài gòn how close the enemy could be to us without fear of being destroyed. This was brought home to us even more inside the Citadel, as the NVA would allow our Marines to close within 20 meters before popping out of their spider holes and opening up with intense automatic weapons fire. This would then be followed by volleys of their B40 rockets. They, in effect, negated our artillery and, in some cases, our close air support. Of course, weather precluded most of our air support, which the enemy knew ahead of time. Our battalion mortars, had we brought them, could have helped in this situation by giving us close in cover, as we pulled back far enough to call in heavy artillery, capable of destroying the enemy. We could only carry so much when we left Sài gòn, and we thought the 57mm recoilless rifle would be more useful in a built-up area. In fact, we needed both. The more destruction we wrought, the easier it was for the enemy to conceal himself. So the type of fire support became a trade-off, and decisions had to be made.

The wall surrounding the Citadel could have been a distinct advantage for us by making it easy to seal off everyone inside. But in our case, the NVA got to the wall first, and were able to defend against us by digging in, under, and down to protect themselves from artillery and bombs, while we had to continually expose ourselves to attack them. They were also able to continuously resupply themselves through the gates they controlled. Their bunkers, foxholes, and trench network must have taken many days to prepare and made it possible for them to defend in any direction and cover every avenue of approach. Our 57mm and 106mm recoilless rifles were usually not enough, unless we hit a bull's eye, to knock out their bunkers. Tear gas worked initially, but the next time we tried it, the enemy had gas masks. Tanks were an option, but trying to get the tank in a position to fire without having it blown up was a real challenge.

5 MAR 68

We have orders to move in the morning. I've just finished going over the operation with my counterpart. I think our relationship is working okay right now, but it got a little strained in the Citadel when I pushed him pretty hard to be more offensive. This operation will be in two phases, two days each. We still have the 1st and 5th Battalions in our task force and will be doing area sweeps using one battalion as a blocking force.

Bill Fite is sick again. He may need to be evacuated before long, before he becomes too weak. His system does not seem to be adapting to the local food. I am still holding up fine and taking my vitamins every day that I can remember.

8 MAR 68

We helo-lifted close to the coast two days ago. There are streams with vegetation, rice paddies, lots of sand, and an occasional village that looks like an oasis. Hué is only a few miles away. We have walked about three miles since landing. The 1st and 5th Battalions to our front have taken a lot of casualties, while we have had only one.

I'm feeling a little down in the dumps right now. Not sure why, but it may be because the other two battalions are having a lot of action and we are just trailing along. I probably should be happy, but I miss not being in the action. Right now we are sitting in a bombed-out village, and I'm watching the other battalion advisors work the helo gunships and artillery up and down the far tree line. My thought is that my counterpart is not trusted by the task force commander. Our company commanders are great, but it takes leadership to let them excel. If I am right, then my gut reaction in Bồng Sơn was right on, and I still have a lot of work to do.

9 MAR 68

The operation is almost over. We have moved again and are back across the Perfume River from Huế. My cowboy, Chiến, returned today, having recovered from the nasty hip wound that he received in Sài gòn. I have missed him. We received some 60mm mortar rounds from the VC this evening. They interrupted my washing from a local well. It felt so refreshing that I finished my bath before taking cover . . . just in time to call in a medevac helo for one of our wounded Marines.

These Marines are wonderful. Our best Boy Scout troops could learn a lot from them. They are truly self-sufficient. Most Americans would be horrified to watch them prepare a meal. I know I've described it earlier, but if you had not seen it being prepared, you might equate the result with a nice US restaurant entree. Most of it is delicious. Of course, you have to realize that I have been eating fresh pig, chicken, or fish, and leafy green vegetables, along with our rice, since we left the Citadel. Anything that is running loose is fair game! We need to eat before dark because any cooking fires will attract unwanted ordnance! I just had a canteen full of soup made with green sprouts and several small fish floating in it. Everything was cooked and had a delicious flavor. Of course, the rice with soy sauce followed. I expect a hot cup of coffee later.

We are not finished with this operation and will head somewhere else tomorrow.

11 MAR 68

It is a beautiful morning. We are a little north of Huế on a small peninsula winding in and out along the Perfume River. A small Vietnamese boat is heading upriver. The US Navy patrol craft roam around lazily back and forth. The church spire across the river stretching above the tree tops has already sounded Mass. It also rang its bell last night. What a beautiful scene from the seawall. But behind me and reminding me of what has happened, is the carnage from weeks earlier . . . the bombed-out villages, the destruction . . . such a contrast. I could be sitting on a boat ramp back home looking out over the water and the scene would look the same in one direction. Maybe that's what has happened in our country, where so many have it so good. Maybe we only see in one direction.

I remember attending a cocktail party with some old high school friends after returning to the US, having lived the last three years in Vietnam and Thailand. I was approached by one of the wives who challenged me on why I served in Vietnam. As I tried to explain, she called me a liar. It stopped the party momentarily. That was my homecoming parade!

The water is like glass. Later, it will become slightly choppy as the wind picks up. When the sun gets a little higher and it warms up, I'll go swimming and take a real bath! Bill Fite has just finished and thoroughly enjoyed himself.

My Jeep hasn't caught up with us yet, so we don't have much except the clothes on our back. I still haven't been paid since I left Đà nẵng. I'm hoping my pay record is straightened out by the time we get back to Sài gòn. Meanwhile, I continue to be indebted to the Cố vấn (advisor) slush fund, which is paying for my food.

Yesterday I traded some of my NVA gear to two Navy Chief Petty Officers for C-rations and coffee. They were passing by on their big fiberglass speedboat with twin 50 caliber machine guns on the bow. I thought it would be a great boat to water ski behind some other time. The goodies are for my US Marine artillery Forward Observer team, who have been with us for a while. One of them can't handle the Vietnamese food.

My latest batch of letters from home are only dated in February. I look forward to them so much, but from the early newspaper clippings I've received about the Tết Offensive, it sounds like we're losing the war. We had some tough battles over the last few weeks, but I thought we won all of them?

Little did I know at the time, but this was the beginning of the end.

12 MAR 68

Capt Vuong invited me to dinner yesterday. We had fresh boiled shrimp, bought from a passing boat, which we dipped in lime juice, salt, and pepper. They were delicious, of course. We also had more bác sĩ để, their whiskey. It appears to be a rice wine mixed with honey. A little bit is okay and I'm willing to indulge for the shrimp! Times like this make me want to believe that I'm making progress with my counterpart. Perhaps it's because everything seems so peaceful and quiet for now. The last few months have been an emotional and stressful roller coaster for all of us. I am still happy and content with my tour in Vietnam, but I need to be more careful in what I wish for when times are slow! Maj Budd is back from R&R and visited us today. He brought us a few goodies to munch and seemed very refreshed from his time in Hawaii. I certainly hope so!

16 MAR 68

We are still here in this beautiful spot. Even though there is still sporadic fighting going on, mainly after dark, it is very pleasant during the day. Medevacs are still required almost daily. We flag down the Navy boats each day and ask the operators to tell us what's happening in the rest of the world. Otherwise, we feel like we're in a time warp, and one day is like the next.

Letters from home help a lot. I understand young Bill (*my son*) is reading up a storm in the first grade, and Carolyn (*four years old*) is trying to learn how to take care of her baby sister, Cathy (*almost one year old*).

18 MAR 68

Still here, but we will be moving soon and headed northwest up into the hills. I'll miss watching the sampans go by. Some have a small motor, others are paddled from the rear with a long oar. I heard today that the MAU finally has my pay record from Đà nẵng and it is up to date. There will be a nice paycheck waiting if we ever return to Sài gòn.

19 MAR 68

The word came down to move back inside the Citadel this afternoon while I was swimming and rinsing out my clothes. I left wearing a wet uniform. We are set up along the southwest wall and plan to move into the hills in the morning. Once inside the Citadel, Bill Fite and I were able to find a barber and look almost human again! I ran into Wayne Swenson and Jim Coolican at the MACV compound and they gave me news on other Marines we knew at TBS. Ray Findlay is further north and has lost almost 40 pounds, John Carr has been wounded twice, and Larry McLaughlin is still a company commander.

Chiến outdid himself fixing dinner today. He and his friends dug up some potatoes, which they boiled, cleaned one of the last chickens left in town, and of course, fixed rice with soy sauce. Very good! About the same time, another US Army lieutenant and his Forward Observer team showed up to support us with their artillery on the upcoming operation. But after watching our food being prepared, they quickly disappeared to eat their C-rations!

20 MAR 68

We left the Citadel this morning and are settled on the top of one of the highest hills in the area west of Huế. It's pouring down rain and I'm trying to stay dry under a poncho. It was boiling hot all day, and the rain has a nice cooling effect for now, but I'm sure the temperature will drop tonight.

24 MAR 68

I'm still on a mountaintop looking out over the valleys, which stretch toward the Perfume River. Today is the first day we haven't moved since the beginning of the operation. Even with the heat, I prefer to move rather than sit. No contact yet, and I don't expect any since we can see for miles. The US Army 101st Airborne Division has units on either side of us so that we each cover for the other. An airplane with a trained Air Observer flying twice a day could probably accomplish our mission much easier than we are.

Bill Fite has been sick for two days and has started to pass blood. I requested a medevac and replacement for him today, but he assured me that he was much better and asked me to wait one more day. Since tomorrow is our last day and we will be flying back to Hué, I agreed. But he must have a medical checkup when we return. We have had too many advisors get sick over here. Not sure what the problem is or why I've been so fortunate. In the meantime, a replacement for Bill Fite arrived on the mail helo.

This afternoon, my counterpart tried to coordinate a pair of US helos without telling me ahead of time. He fouled it up, and I had to intervene. Needless to say, he lost some face. If he had just let me know in time, I could have helped him through the process. Nevertheless, I feel like we are getting along. He brought me an ice-cold beer yesterday from an ARVN resupply helo. It really tasted good since it feels like 110 degrees up here, and I haven't had anything cold to drink since we left Sài gòn. However, I'm still getting by with one canteen of water per day on each operation.

We should be back in Hué tomorrow, and then I think we may be headed back to Vũng Tàu where we were before the NVA so rudely attacked everywhere! I have four days growth of beard, which is almost bleached white from the sun, and I am looking forward to getting cleaned up. It has gotten dark and I'm under my poncho with a small penlight hooked to a radio battery, trying to write . . . and, of course, it's raining again!

25 MAR 68

Well, the helo ride back was canceled, so I sent Bill Fite back by medevac helo and the 4th Battalion started walking toward Huế.

26 MAR 68

We finished walking back to Huế today as orders from TF changed many times. The latest is that we will head back to Sài gòn tomorrow.

8

The main part of our battalion flew back to Sài gòn yesterday and we are positioned on the eastern edge of town as part of the CMD (Command Military District) defense. The rest of the battalion caught up with us today. As usual, the flights were scrambled and not well coordinated. My personal gear is now spread between three locations.

An MAU representative was waiting for me when I landed last night and told me that HQMC is planning to send me to Thailand after Vietnam . . . I'm going to be assigned with family to a joint service Hq in Bangkok for two years. I'm anxious to find out more about it, even though it won't happen until October.

The joint service Hq would be USMACTHAI (the US Military Assistance Command, Thailand), staffed by US military from all services.

I drove to the MAU today and had a long talk with Col Michael. He concurs with my evaluation of my counterpart and will support my recommendations. Also, when things settle down around here, if they ever do, Col Michael said he would send me to Bangkok for a weekend to find out more about my new job. That could be very helpful in our Woodbridge planning, such as when to sell the house, the car, the boat, what to put in stowage, when to pull young Bill out of school . . . and how and when I might get home before we have to leave for Bangkok?

Meanwhile, something is in the wind for our next operation. The 2nd and 3rd Battalions have moved down to the Mekong Delta in IV Corps. We could be next.

1 APR 68

Not much happening here right now. Gene Gardner and I met some other advisors in downtown Sài gòn and had a steak dinner last night. I couldn't finish it. My stomach has shrunk, but it was really good!

There are still VC being reported close by, but they seem to vanish before we can react. Mostly, we just sit around and sweat. It is very hot during the day, and when the sun goes down, the mosquitoes come out. Haven't heard any confirmation on where we go next. With this lull in activity, I have caught up on all my reports.

My substitute cowboy while Chiến was hurt, Ba, invited me to dinner with his wife this evening. It was a nice Vietnamese dinner and I appreciated their hospitality.

2 APR 68

I'm sleeping on a porch with a cool evening breeze that helps keep the bugs away. The sky is clear, and the stars are beautiful. It's been hard to stop thinking about Bangkok, but I'm sure that will end as soon as we start another operation.

4 APR 68

We leave in the morning at 4 am for a boat ride and an amphibious landing along the Sài gòn River. Gene and the 6th Battalion will fly in by helo and be a blocking force. We flew a helo reconnaissance earlier, and the area looks very soggy. I'll have a US Navy photographer and a journalist with me on this operation. That should prove interesting.

We were told today that we are moving back to Vũng Tàu next week for some recovery time, and then down to the Delta to operate with the MRF (Maritime Riverine Force). I'm looking forward to that. It will help the time fly by.

5 APR 68

We're back from the operation. There were no enemy contacts, but I enjoyed riding in the boat, landing on a beach, and wading across streams up to my chest. It will take another day for all my gear to dry.

I just heard over the radio that Dr. King was assassinated. How sad. I remember that President Kennedy was assassinated the last time I was overseas. Maybe the news will stop complaining about Vietnam for a few days.

6 APR 68

The news sounds like there is looting and rioting in city streets over Dr. King's death. Maybe the rioters should be drafted if they're looking for violence. There's plenty of that over here!

My date for R&R is going to be 13 May. I'm ready now! Everyone that has been says Honolulu is great. Right now, the two best things about being back in Sài gòn are mail every day and church on Sunday. But that will end next week.

8 APR 68

We leave on trucks for Vũng Tàu in the morning. I will be taking a case of poison ivy with me. It showed up after our last operation and I can't seem to dry it up. Maybe some salt water and sun in Vũng Tàu will help.

9 APR 68—*written from Vũng Tàu*

We arrived today after a long Jeep ride. I've already visited with some of my restaurant friends, and they haven't forgotten me. They like Bill Fite, too. There is still an 8 pm curfew, so the town shuts down early.

10 APR 68

Bill and I visited with more Vietnamese friends today and were invited to lunch by one of our Marines. Later, I toured the battalion enlisted camp and, after talking with Captain Vuong, decided they needed some supplies. Using my Jeep, Bill and I located what they needed and took a couple of Jeep loads to them. This afternoon a Vietnamese Navy man invited me to his home and presented me with one of their black berets. I appreciated his thoughtfulness. Vũng Tàu is a very nice place to be in a war-ravaged country.

11 APR 68

Today I managed to get milk and cereal for our enlisted dependents and sent Bill to pick up a load of donated firewood for them to use in their stoves to cook. And I've talked Captain Vuong into approving a well so they will have fresh water. As you can guess, there has been very little concern shown for these folks. They are living in poverty. If we had more time in Vũng Tàu, I know Bill and I could improve their living conditions even more. However, Bill is sick again, and I need to keep a close eye on him.

12 APR 68

I arranged for more food items to be delivered to the battalion dependents today. And I finally arranged to have a phone hooked up in my little office so I can talk to the MAU in Sài gòn. Bill is still not well, but not sick enough to evacuate. He has lost a lot of weight and needs to get well soon if he's going to go south with us.

I've invited two US Army doctors to our battalion party tomorrow, and in exchange, they are going to do some medical checkups on our dependents. I can't change the culture over here overnight, but I can surely help the current situation.

Last night at the hotel, an Army and an Air Force advisor were complaining because their office air conditioners were not cooling the air enough and they were having to work a full day! I had to laugh

. . . and then an Army colonel drove by in his air-conditioned staff car . . . and the war goes on.

13 APR 68

Found out today that next week the battalion will go back to Sài gòn for one day, and then will head south to the Mekong Delta. Bill's Army roommate is now sick. The last time we were in Vũng Tàu, two and one-half months ago, my Army roommate became ill. Interesting!

Captain Vuong took Bill and me to breakfast this morning. Afterward, he called the town mayor and requested that the well be dug for our dependents. Times like this give me hope for their future. To top off the day, the sun is bright and warm with a cool breeze blowing in from the ocean. What a beautiful spot in a war-ravaged country.

Later today I took advantage of an offer from an Army dentist friend to clean and check my teeth. He replaced one filling but otherwise said my teeth were in good shape. Must be the rice! I think this was the least discomfort I can ever remember in a dentist chair.

14 APR 68

Our battalion had a party last night for all the Marines and their families since we are leaving tomorrow for another extended period. We even had a USO show for them, which was pretty good. My counterpart has been especially friendly of late. I am not sure why, but it seems to happen each time I complain to TF Hq and/or Col Michael at MAU Hq. Capt Vuong and the battalion executive officer are due to be promoted to major soon, so it will be interesting to see if the current attitude continues afterward. I'm guessing it won't last long, and I hope I'm wrong.

I just remembered that today is Easter! I hope I can find a Protestant service close by.

9

We're finally set up for the night after bouncing around in the Jeep for eleven hours. We drove to Sài gòn last night and headed south at 7 am this morning. It is very hot down here in the Mekong Delta, but my washcloth bath helped a little.

We will be working for TF B again, as we were for a short time in Sài gòn during Tết. My initial impression of the situation is not good. The advisors here, as in Vũng Tàu, appear to be living the good life. Hope I'm wrong. There are numerous US Army compounds around Cần Thơ with swimming pools, clubs, and post exchanges. I see very little attempt to assimilate with the Vietnamese or help them win the war.

19 APR 68

We left Cần Thơ the morning after we arrived and have been sloshing around in the mud and slime ever since. On the good side, though, there are no hills to climb, and there is an abundance of good food . . . fruits, vegetables, fish, chickens and pigs, and even coconuts when we get thirsty.

The VC down here are tougher fighters than the VC we faced in Bồng Sơn, perhaps because they have been resupplied by the NVA with new equipment and weapons from China. Nevertheless, we have inflicted a lot of casualties, mainly with our artillery, and have only suffered a few wounded. The 3rd Battalion, operating with us, has had a lot more friendly KIA and wounded.

20 APR 68

The other TF advisors went to one of the US clubs for breakfast. It was tempting, but I decided to stay here on the porch of the small house where Capt Vuong and I are staying. A little bit later Capt Vuong invited me to have breakfast with him in town. I was the only US advisor at the restaurant amid the Vietnamese Marines and locals . . . Shades of Vũng Tàu.

I've just read several US newspaper articles about operations that we participated in, and I am amazed at how much the numbers seem to be inflated. It appears that someone has added up everything going on in country and credited it to one operation.

21 APR 68

I went to church this morning. It had been a while, and I was glad to find a chaplain down here. I seem to be more tired lately, especially after our last operation. Not sure what that's about. Maybe I need to exercise more! There is a swimming pool in the Army compound that I'll try out later. Maybe that will help. We are only being sent on small operations about once a week. Higher Hq seems reluctant to commit us for any length of time, perhaps because we have been designated the Reserve for the IV Corps Commander. That means that if any other unit gets in trouble, we will be committed to help them out. The last time this happened was during Tết, when we were committed to reinforce Sài gòn!

Tom Ward, with the 5th Battalion, said he is having some of the same problems trying to coordinate with his counterpart that I've described earlier. I discussed these concerns with Col Michael when I was in Sài gòn and think we might do our job better if we concentrated our advising at the TF level. Without strong reinforcing leadership from the TF Commander, it's hard to make an impact at a lower level.

22 APR 68

We watched an excellent USO show last night . . . much folk singing and guitar playing. I also checked on the availability of a

MARS (Military Auxiliary Radio System) phone patch. It would be nice to confirm R&R plans before heading to Hawaii.

Tomorrow we are scheduled to go out with the RAG (River Assault Group), similar to our last operation in Sài gòn.

24 APR 68

We just finished the RAG operation, and I am exhausted. Maybe it's the heat and fighting the mud and crossing swiftly flowing streams after the RAG boats drop us off. I slipped and sank while crossing one stream, but a couple of Marines behind me grabbed the barrel of my carbine, which was slung over my shoulder, pulled me up, and got me moving again. Most of our Marines build a small raft out of bamboo or tie up their stuff in a poncho to float and swim their gear across. One of these Marines was swept away, and it took several of us to get him back. Another one became stuck in the mud bottom due to suction, and it took 15 minutes to pull him free.

We had three VC KIAs last night in an ambush we had set up. We also captured their weapons and a stash of papers. There are large groups of VCs in our vicinity, but they seem to always be one step ahead.

26 APR 68

Bill is still having some stomach problems. Poor guy! He fights it hard, but it won't quite go away. I'm still holding up well, but can't shake the tired feeling. Maybe I need some iron pills.

Here are a few more details on what we did in Vũng Tàu . . . we arranged the well for the dependents through CORDS (Connecting Organizations for Regional Disease Surveillance) and USAID (US Agency for International Development) and then had Capt V call the Mayor and request it. We arranged for MEDCAP (Medical Civil Action Program) from the local US Army hospital to visit and treat the dependents twice a week.

The latest rumor from Sài gòn is that I will move up to be the TF B advisor in July. There will be several new advisors arriving around that time.

Due to several factors, that would not happen.

27 APR 68

Last night I tried to call home on a MARS but wasn't able to get through. I'll try again another night. Our mail left Sài gòn a week ago and is still not here. It's only a 45-minute plane ride. I hope it isn't lost!

Things are very slow right now. I'm going to the pool to swim and then play basketball while I can. My quarters are excellent right now. Bill and I are sharing a small house next to Capt Vuong.

We are having breakfast together every morning. All is well again. My on-again-off-again relationship with him has never been better. Wish I could say the same for the other advisors. It may have something to do with him hearing that I might be moving to the TF Hq . . . and being able to influence his boss! I am going to ask Tom and his counterpart to join us for breakfast. And if that works, I'll ask the TF counterparts to join us. It's worth a try.

Gene's 6th Battalion, up in Sài gòn, was in a pretty good fight the other day, but Gene wasn't part of it. His assistant Brad was. He was the Captain who relieved me in Sài gòn when I was evacuated to the hospital. Gene is disappointed that he missed the action, of course, and I can understand. Although he has been with his battalion almost six months longer than I've been with the 4th Battalion, we have had a lot more action.

For whatever reason the Lord has watched over me since I arrived and not only has placed me in harm's way but has allowed me to weather the storm. He has been there to conquer my fears, as well as given me the strength to persevere. I don't enjoy watching people die or get hurt. I don't enjoy the destruction. But we are trained to fight and to win when our country calls on us. Once a battle begins, it is easy to get caught up with the tide of excitement, tenseness, and efficiency necessary to win. It's not until later, after a prolonged lull, that depression sets in and I begin to wonder what I've been about.

It does no good to attempt to weigh the good and the bad. There is no good, and I reject the bad in order to live with myself. Perhaps it would be better never to be involved in a big battle, but only someone who has been there can say that with any certainty. How else could a Marine know? The ultimate goal of all of our training, the true test of worth to one's self and his unit is the battlefield. Until it happens, we can only wonder how we might react, not really knowing, but always preparing just the same.

Not so with our junior officers today. They are not fortunate enough to have been subjected to the long waiting period of preparation as we were. They are immediately immersed into the cauldron of combat, the very heart of our Corps, most while they are still lieutenants. They discover early in their careers whether or not they have what it takes, and fortunately, most do. If perchance they are not tested fully on their first tour here, they still have a whole career to find out.

However, for Gene, myself, Charlie, and others in our group, it is different. Our careers are suddenly half over and the tremendous psychological preparation, as well as the many years of professional preparation, can seem wasted unless we are afforded an opportunity to be tested. Of course, we still feel patriotism and devotion to our homeland, and I'm sure we always will. But Gene's innate desire to be tested in combat is very real and very personal in all of us.

Happy birthday to Cathy. Next to Christmas, I think I miss birthdays the most.

28 APR 68

The weather is beautiful today, although it rained hard for about an hour. The monsoon season has arrived, and the monsoon rains will keep coming. I went to church this morning, but don't like it as well as the one in Sài gòn.

It looks like we will probably stay around here until May Day before we start operating again. There is a lot of intelligence pointing toward another NVA offensive. Not sure why they would want to do that again.

Years later, it would become evident to me that the NVA were not only winning the war of attrition back then, but they were also starting to win the war of US public opinion.

From April 29 to May 8, we continued to go on small operations, sometimes as a battalion, sometimes with just one company. Bill would go on the smaller ops while I stayed back and monitored the op over the radio. During this time, we had several wounded from mortar attacks and booby traps. The medevac helos were not always responsive, resulting in a few KIAs. At the same time, we were also inflicting enemy WIAs and KIAs and picking up a few weapons.

On May 6, I started to have cramps for the first time in-country. Two days later, I began passing blood. Fortunately, I was picked up by helo on the 10th and flown back to Sài gòn on the 11th to prepare for my R&R flight to Honolulu on the 14th. By then, I had recovered from my intestinal problem and had a most enjoyable reunion with Pat until I returned to Sài gòn on the 20th.

10

—*written from Sài gòn*

Arrived back in-country yesterday afternoon. R&R was wonderful. It was tremendous!

I was back in Sài gòn before Pat took off from Honolulu!

I was not able to make connections after we landed, so I spent yesterday and today reorganizing my stuff and catching up on paperwork. Gene drove in and had dinner with me last night. He had a little action while I was gone, and his spirits are up. He has been promoted to Major.

I'll fly back down south in the morning. I'm ready to go back to the battalion and yet I dread it at the same time. There is so much our battalion could be doing rather than sitting and waiting to react. Talked with Col Michael again about moving up to TF B and he has decided that the situation with my counterpart is such that I can do more good by staying with the 4th Battalion until I rotate.

23 MAY 68—*written from somewhere outside Cần Thơ*

After waiting four hours, my plane finally took off and landed in Cần Thơ. I then boarded a helo with our TF B mail and landed somewhere. I'll figure it out later. Everyone was happy to get mail! Bill left on the helo to have a medical check-up. Capt John Burke, who filled in for me while I was on R&R, stayed on to cover for Bill.

We have a small company-size operation today, which John can cover. I'll stay at our battalion CP. Don't know how long we will be here in no-man's-land or even when I can mail this letter. If I sound a little grim, it's because it is grim! I am adjusting from R&R as quickly as I can, but it isn't easy. I am slowly starting to speak Vietnamese again and eat their food, but it is a little harder this time, compared to when I first joined the battalion. I am not miserable, but certainly not comfortable yet . . . and I'm still mentally tired.

27 MAY 68

Just returned from a one-day operation that lasted four days. Details later. A helo is flying in to drop off Bill and pick up John and I want to mail this short letter to let you know I'm fine.

28 MAY 68

On the 23rd, we moved out suddenly at noon and returned at dark. The following morning, we left suddenly again at 7:30 for another one-day operation. That evening we changed direction and were ordered to remain overnight. We had a helo resupply of chow and spent the next two days stumbling around and changing from one direction to the next. We spent most of the time in mud and water, sometimes up to our necks. Our feet only got dry at night when we pulled off boots and socks and watched the mosquitos swarm. I slept on banana leaves, drank boiled canal-water, and ate rice for four days. We also were able to pick a few coconuts and fruit to eat. Tom's 5th Battalion was also with us.

While we were gone, the VC fired mortars into the compound we had just left and wounded our stay-behind element plus a few dependents that had joined us from Vũng Tàu.

Finally, after I was convinced we were on a wild goose chase, the VC surprised us with a perfect "L"-shaped ambush and engaged two of our lead companies, both of whom started taking immediate casualties. John was pinned down immediately and was up to his neck in water for several hours. My counterpart was calling for ARVN artillery fire support, and I was trying to coordinate an air strike. The VC had moved in so close to us that our friendly artillery rounds were landing behind them! This turned out to be a good thing because it cut off their escape route. They fired a lot of B-40 rockets and automatic weapons at us, making it hard for me to get in a position where I could see. I was across the stream from John but could see enough to know we had to break the VC attack or suffer many more casualties. After more than an hour of continuous fire support, I was able to slowly adjust an air strike right up to our front lines and had a direct hit on the VC! We didn't hear anything but a few scattered shots from that time on. That night we had a few more scattered B-40 and mortar rounds from some distance away.

I'm guessing we ran into about half of a VC battalion and Tom's 5th Battalion ran into the other half but that the VC quickly disengaged and got away. The next day an ARVN battalion in a blocking position finished the job for us. We were only able to find 30 enemy KIA and 15 weapons, but there were many body bits and pieces in the vicinity of our air strikes. Additionally, I'm sure the VC drug away many bodies and buried them during the night.

We suffered many casualties as well due to the ambush but still have a viable fighting unit. I had trouble getting timely helo medical evacuation, a continual problem.

At one point, I had to wave off a medevac helo rather than risk having it shot down. We were still receiving small arms and mortar fire. As a result, I saw a Marine's arm amputated with a large knife and a pair of scissors! We only had a little morphine and glucose with us . . . no qualified surgeon. Those guys were so brave.

Didn't think it was possible, but I again saw and experienced more than I ever want to again. The streams and canals are so strong down here that we lost one Marine trying to cross . . . and never found him. War is not nice, anyway you look at it.

The ARVN Corps Commander is flying in this afternoon to present awards to our Marines for their bravery. They deserve it.

29 MAY 68

We are preparing to move tomorrow to another area close by. I hope it isn't quite as wet. My uniforms are literally rotting off of me. I'm almost down to my skivvies (underwear).

30 MAY 68

My spirits are much higher today. I like our new location better than our last. It is still pouring down rain, but I have a good roof over my head and a dry place to sleep. A gentle breeze blows through most of the time. We still have a dirt floor and the requisite number of bugs, but they're not bad.

I'm eating with my counterpart again. We've been at odds over this for a while. Chiến has been cooking for me since we moved down here, and not doing a very good job. I've mentioned it to Maj Vuong. Additionally, on our last operation, I needed a battery for my radio and asked our battalion supply officer for a replacement. I had just arranged for the battalion to receive a large resupply and thought asking for one of their batteries was a reasonable request, but I was refused twice. So, I refused to provide any US support for the rest of the day . . . and I informed TF Hq.

I had a new battery first thing in the morning, and now Maj Vuong and I are eating together again! This issue has gone back and forth since our time in Huế.

31 MAY 68

Today I counseled Chiến and Mạnh. They had eased up in their duties to take care of me. It didn't take much and they both improved. I think it's the weather . . . continual rain, and too much sitting around.

I've started to read Atlas Shrugged and like it. It helps pass the time.

The nearby stream is too filthy to swim in, but I do splash around in order to live with myself. After all, we do drink the water . . . after it's boiled!

1 JUN 68

Another month has arrived, and we are still in the same spot. Maj Vuong and I are scheduled to fly to TF Hq tomorrow, and I'm hoping it will include a future operation briefing. At the very least, I'll be able to send out my letters.

Our Marines are climbing palm trees and cutting down some of the coconuts. The milk is tasty and a welcome change from water and tea.

2 JUN 68

We flew to TF Hq today and were not briefed on any future operations. Guess we'll stay where we are for a while longer. Worse than that, we still are not receiving any mail. That was a real downer.

3 JUN 68

Just finished dinner with Maj Vuong and I'm still amazed at what these cooks can turn out with a couple of old pots over a campfire. Tonight, we had rice (of course), noodle soup with onion sprouts, fried pork, omelet with peppers, boiled eggs, and a fresh banana. They sprinkle sugar over the pork when they fry it. Delicious!

I wake up each morning in my hammock with the sunrise in my eyes. It is beautiful.

4 JUN 68

We had a surprise one-day operation today. It was uneventful. But at least we got up and did something.

Our CP area is starting to look and smell like a garbage dump! I'll suggest to Maj Vuong tomorrow that we need to do some field hygiene.

5 JUN 68

I'm beginning to think that this is really a bad war for everybody at every level. But I could not have stayed out of it and lived with myself. I continue to see so many things that are just not right. It's hard to be a part of obvious mistakes. Striving for excellence seems to be a minority thought. I just heard on the radio about the RFK assassination. It's hard to understand what's happening here and back in the US.

Supper time ... omelet, meat, rice, soup, bananas, and Vietnamese plums. My highlight of the day. I can understand and appreciate this.

12 JUN 68

Happy birthday yesterday. I hope it was a good day for you. We haven't had any enemy contacts since my last letter, but we have been on constant operations. We left unexpectedly on 6 June for an extended operation. All of our personal gear was sent back to a battalion rear area and we headed south in a convoy by Jeep. That evening, since we had not had any enemy contact, we were flown back by helo to where we had started. So there we were, back in our camp with only what we had carried with us that morning . . . no stationery, no battery lights to read or write after dark, etc. We went on two more ops before we finally caught up with our personal gear again. But then we were immediately sent back on the same op we had just run . . . without our personal gear again!

About this time Bill and I were listening to the US Army battalion advisors on their radio frequency, who were ordering their daily resupply of C-rations, water, and beer. They operate in groups of three or four, unlike our Marine concept of assigning one advisor with the Battalion Commander and one with the lead Company Commander . . . a totally different concept.

A couple of days ago I had an unpleasant encounter with an Army advisor as we were about to be extracted by helo and flown back to base camp. He was trying to control our extraction from a helo above us. While I was waist deep in mud, in between trying to cross canals as fast as I could in order to reach the LZ, this guy was giving me detailed instructions that sounded like a formal parade ceremony directive! Bill, with our lead company, had arrived at the designated LZ half-an-hour before me and had begun to organize our Marines in accordance with the SOP for this Army Corps. They are all different. Apparently, Bill's efforts did not meet the standard of our young controller in the sky, so he began to repeat himself with detailed instructions saying we must comply.

At this point, I was trying to balance on a single log across a mud bog, but fell off, dragging my radio operator with me! Nevertheless, I tried to reply by reassuring this guy that our battalion routinely conducted helo operations and that we would make this work. But he refused to give up and kept repeating his instructions to me like some character out of "The General".

Having realized early on that this guy was not in command of anybody or anything but was merely just another coordinator like us, I cordially invited him to land and personally pace off the twenty paces he insisted were required between our battalion helo teams! For some reason, this seemed to upset the young man. Nevertheless, he directed the helos to land, but 180 degrees from where we needed them, causing mass confusion for about five minutes. By this time, I had the LZ in sight and was wading up to set things straight, when I tried to cross another mud bog and promptly sank out of sight! I'll end here because it didn't get much better. We did finally get aboard the helos and returned to our base camp . . . tired, wet, muddy, bedraggled, looking every bit like combat Marines.

Yesterday was very much the same thing all over again minus the helicopter ride. We just walked and swam more. It would be hard to imagine what this Mekong Delta is really like without experiencing it. Most of the bridges have been destroyed. Many of the canals and streams require a raft to cross. Our Marines make them by lashing bamboo logs together. The currents are so strong sometimes that we often land as far as fifty yards downstream from where we launch. The difference between low and high tide can be over my head. This causes some of the mud bogs I've mentioned to be as deep as four or five feet.

Also, yesterday we watched B-52s drop 1000-pound bombs on an area where an Army Ranger battalion had taken heavy casualties the day before, and then we walked into what was left. I've never seen anything as devastated. It was very depressing. I wondered how many years it would take for the land to be viable again.

One of the more surprising things I've run across down here are the ruins and almost intact homes we stumble over or literally run into the middle of the jungle. Once abandoned, it only takes a few months to lose an entire hamlet to the overgrowth. I've walked across stone foundations of homes that were much larger than what we are used to back in the States. I'm sure they must have been French villas during the French Indochina days.

13 JUN 68

Forgot to mention that on our last enemy contact I called in an air strike and had them fire rockets and drop bombs just across the canal from where we were pinned down. Maj Vuong stayed very close to me on that mission! I think he is slowly realizing that he still has a lot to learn about coordinating supporting arms.

15 JUN 68

Yesterday morning, we were alerted to go on another operation. The 3rd Battalion was our blocking force. From 7 am to 7 pm, I was ankle deep, waist deep, or neck deep in water, mud, and slime. We managed to flush a small group of VC. I called in a pair of helo gunships, and we ended up with two enemy KIA, a 60mm French mortar with a few rounds of ammo, and some other VC equipment. The mortar was in an area that Tom and I had suspected.

By taking a back azimuth from where some earlier mortar rounds had landed, we were able to predict where the mortars had been fired.

Later we were ordered back to our old location in order to protect Cần Thơ. This is really getting old. What a rut we've fallen into.

16 JUN 68

I think it's Sunday again. We have moved back into our old compound, which is depressing . . . but I've just eaten a fresh pineapple. That helped.

US Army MGen Eckhardt and the VN IV Corps Commander stopped by yesterday afternoon. The general complained that the Marines were moving too slowly on our last operation. I tried to explain that we would have sacrificed security to move any faster in all that "muck!" Then I asked if I could speak off the record, and told him what I thought of our mission. He listened but did not seem to appreciate my honesty! His aide was a young Army captain standing erect with an M-79 grenade launcher at the ready. He seemed so nervous that I was afraid that if anyone raised their voice unexpectedly, he might crank off a round accidentally before we could stop him!

We've been down here in the Delta 60 days now and we've been on operations 27 of those days, which means either we were soaking wet and muddy or we were bored stiff.

Our mail is still sporadic in arriving, from a few days to more than a week. Don't know why there is such a problem delivering it from Sài gòn. There is a rumor that we may be going on a big operation soon. We will see.

17 JUN 68

No operations for three days, so Maj Vuong and I took a boat ride into Cần Thơ yesterday and went to TF HQ . . . best part of trip was picking up our mail.

19 JUN 68

We started out yesterday on a typical "see how far we can trudge through the mud" day. Sometime after we had left, it was decided to send us back home. We were too far to walk back but decided to try anyway. About 11 pm we were ordered to halt for the night. We had walked as far as the old position where we used to be, but the 3rd Battalion was there now. We had one Marine drown crossing a stream. His sampan was swamped by the medevac helo that I had called in for another Marine, who had been shot in the stomach by a sniper. Unfortunately, he also died . . . not a good day.

During our walk back, I coordinated illumination flare drops from an Air Force C-47 aircraft that we call "Spooky," so we could see where we were going. It was too dangerous for us to be strung out in the dark, dead tired, trying to cross canals and mud bogs one after another. We had been moving since early morning, and our Marines were starting to fall out. I couldn't blame them. I felt like it myself. These little guys have amazing endurance down here . . . better, I think, then some of our US Marine units, and better than they had performed earlier in the mountains up north.

The longer I'm here, the more I appreciate life and the opportunities that come with it. Although it is a sacrifice to be over here, it takes freedom to really appreciate life, and no sacrifice is too great for freedom.

Last night I reprimanded my counterpart for insisting that I commit all kinds of US air support to cover our proposed walk back in the dark, and then, after I coordinated all of it, he changed his mind halfway back and stopped! I got my point across without ever raising my voice. It was almost more than he could handle, but this morning we were OK again. I don't think my counterpart is comfortable being challenged on his use of supporting arms. I haven't been relieved yet, and I believe I'm right in trying to teach them how to best use the support available, be it Vietnamese or US. I make no attempt to buy my way into their friendship other than to accept them for who they are, eat their food, live with them, and help with advice when they ask for it . . . and when they need US support, give them everything I can get! I've refused to ask for US support several times when Vietnamese support was available and adequate. This seemed to come as a big shock!

I have figured out on the map that we walked more than 11 miles yesterday in the mud and water, except for one mile of rocky trail close to the river. I continue to be amazed at the stamina of these little people with these huge packs. It certainly is embarrassing for an advisor and the MAU when a cố vấn is not in decent shape when he arrives here to advise. Bill's replacement was not, and it showed. When we were attacked crossing the stream yesterday, John was too tired to climb out, and it did not go unnoticed!

The same general who had visited us earlier, the IV Corps Commander, arrived by helo shortly after we returned and wanted to tell Maj Vuong and me that he had agreed with our comments during his earlier visit. As a result, the 4th Battalion is being given our own TAOR (Tactical Area of Operations), in other words, our own area to operate in independently. My faith in the system is slowly being restored.

I put a letter on the General's helo that I had been carrying through the muck for two days in a plastic bag, hoping that I would find someone to mail it for me. Unfortunately, the plastic leaked and my letter may be hard to read.

Fortunately, the letter was readable, as I have discovered fifty years later.

20 JUN 68

Mail call . . . with a box of goodies! I appreciate the fruit-flavored drink mixes. Mixing them with boiled water from the streams is a real treat. The candy, on the other hand, melts all over everything before it ever reaches us in the Delta. The same thing happened to the cheese spread. Popcorn is a winner, and we will pop it over a fire as soon as things settle down. We leave on a three-day op with the 3rd Battalion tomorrow, so I need to start preparing.

24 JUN 68

We are back, and this operation was harder to believe than any of the others! The Vietnamese AF were going to helo lift us back just before dark, but were called off by the general who has visited us twice. Then we were told to start walking back toward the highway we had left six hours earlier . . . in the dark! We finally linked up with some Vietnamese trucks at Phụng Hiệp and they carried us 18 miles back to Cần Thơ. From there, we walked back to where we had started two days before, arriving about 8:15 last night.

Needless to say, this is getting old fast. Our young Marines are feeling it the hardest. I feel better moving rather than just sitting in one location, but the senseless nature of it all bothers me a lot. We did capture four VC and a weapon the first day, while Tom's 3rd Battalion got nothing.

On the good side, our initial helo lift to begin the op went smoothly. I had to counsel Maj Vuong again, this time on throwing the smoke grenade in the landing zone too late for the pilots to see which way the wind was blowing. (*I didn't tell him of my earlier tear gas grenade incident back in Bồng Sơn! Perhaps I should have.*)

He got excited again about being corrected and raised his voice, even though he knew he had made a mistake. I did not but continued to talk in a normal tone, which was almost more than he could bear. Raising your voice over here in a discussion is considered a sign of weakness, but he doesn't seem able to control himself. However, we still get along very well in between these eruptions and continue to discuss things. I believe Maj Vuong is fairly competent but is lacking a few leadership traits in order to be a successful commander. He is still too arrogant, self-concerned, and sometimes just plain lazy.

This last op consisted of moving 16 miles in a relatively straight line . . . not very tactical or innovative, nor making use of the elaborate overlays that were provided by higher headquarters. We killed several pigs and chickens along the way, however, so we ate well. Maybe my counterpart is smarter than I think he is.

I can't remember if I've mentioned the children's reaction to me on these operations. More often than not, I'm usually with only one or two Vietnamese Marines when I move through a village or built-up area. Most of these areas down here have seen few, if any, US troops. Some children cry and run when they see me. Others laugh and some point at me in amazement. They usually don't recognize that I'm different until I'm almost next to them, which catches them by surprise when they see my face. It always bothers me to have a child cry and be afraid as I pass by. I'm sure part of their reaction is associated with the destruction we have caused to so many of their homes and families. The older folks well know the devastation that we cannot help but cause when we come under attack, but I'm sure it's hard for a child to comprehend. In some cases, it may be hard for all to understand. War is not fair.

My tiger suit uniform is disintegrating in this heat and moisture. I've tried to have it repaired and reinforced, but on this last op, the legs split and frayed beyond repair. I only have two sets with me down here, and both trousers are worn out. I am wearing my tiger shorts now and am okay on ops, because we are in the mud or water most of the time, but am reluctant to visit headquarters without a complete uniform to wear. I've requested help from Sài gòn, but it will take time for them to have more made for me.

My mind is about to explode! I'm sharing a bunker with Maj Vuong, all of his tactical radios, his tape recorder, and his personal radio. The noise is such that I can barely hear my own tactical radio when someone calls. I need to leave from time to time and find Bill, who is close by for a change, and try to find a little peace of mind.

25 JUN 68

We have another 24-hour op tomorrow starting with a helo lift. Our Marines at this point are really tired and starting to drag, understandably so. Twenty percent of them are down with immersion foot problems and/or sickness. It continues to get worse. The monsoon season is in full swing, causing it to rain often and very hard, leaving us wet most of the time. We will be too far to walk back tomorrow and once again, there is no plan to get us back to base camp before dark. The weather has started to cool off quickly as the storms pass over us. I actually shivered a few times on the last op when we stopped moving. In between the storms, however, it is almost too hot to sleep.

I heard from Tom today that our Task Force HQ has our mail, but has been unable to schedule a delivery to us. Well, at least the mail has left Sài gòn . . . one step at a time.

I start each of these operations hoping for success with no friendly casualties, but I know the chances are slim and things will be chaotic by the end of the day as we try to rush madly for home base. I will be going on the op in shorts tomorrow. I no longer have any long trousers to wear, and TF hasn't figured out how to resupply me. There will be many of our troops in the same fix, and some don't even have boots! This issue will be a highlight in my after-tour report!

It has gotten so hard to move through the mud that I don't even carry a canteen anymore. I only carry my carbine, a compass, and a waterproof map. When I really get thirsty, my cowboy cuts down a coconut, and I drink from it. This is like a different world compared to my time up in I Corps with the US Marines.

27 JUN 68

Bill will try to hitch a boat ride to Cần Thơ today to pick up our mail and try to find some trousers for me.

The op went better yesterday. We arrived back in base camp before dark. The helo lifts went well for a change except, as we began the helo lift, the VC harassed us by firing B-40 rocket rounds and rifle grenades. They caused a few friendly casualties before we chased them away with helicopter gunships, which resulted in three VC KIA. We are also suffering wounded from booby traps on almost a daily basis.

My shorts worked out quite well yesterday. There were a few laughs, but my agility was greatly increased moving in and out of the many canals, bogs, and rice paddies. Bill still has one good pair of trousers, but Tom has also worn through his last pair.

Yesterday I coordinated my first night Vietnamese helo medevac. A 60mm mortar round had exploded prematurely and wounded several Marines, two seriously. It took almost four hours for the helicopter to arrive . . . and then, as I tried to guide the pilot into a landing zone with a flashlight, he drifted across our compound, blowing everything away, and almost crashed into a tree, our command bunker, and a wall. It was a real nightmare! We did accomplish the mission, finally, but I'm sure one Marine will lose his leg and the other Marine will probably not survive due to loss of blood caused by the delay. I feel so helpless in these situations.

Happy birthday to Carolyn. I wish I could be there.

29 JUN 68

Yesterday Bill brought back mail and a pair of trousers for me to wear, so today I took a boat into Cần Thơ and met Tom for lunch. He had only been back from R&R a few days and, of course, really enjoyed it. He saw Gene in Sài gòn and said Gene was much happier now that his tour was almost over!

The latest letter I received yesterday was mailed on 18 June. I wish it didn't take so long, but on the other hand, I should be happy to get any mail down here in the Delta. The challenge now is to hope our mail arrives without getting soaked and then to keep it dry long enough to read. All the pictures mailed from home are arriving stuck together.

I guess I missed wishing Fathers' Day to our Dads. I don't even know when it was!

I've now reached the point when I can no longer stand the loud noise from all of my counterpart's radios; I just go outside and stand in the rain for a while. I'm still fine, though, just blowing off a little steam.

The rain is getting worse each day, and it has been non-stop since last night. We are only doing local ops because most of the area is now flooded. The mosquitoes are about to take over. So glad we have a mosquito net for our cots.

1 JUL 68

Another month has gone by. We have moved back to our original location outside of Cần Tho. The good news is that I'm finally out of that bunker with all the noise. The not-so-good news is that I'm back to sleeping in a hammock under a partial roof with a poncho strung up to keep the rain from blowing in on me.

We've gone four days without a battalion-size operation, although we are sending out separate companies. Therefore, Bill is still having to wade through all the muck with each one of them.

2 JUL 68

We are scheduled for a battalion operation tomorrow. Bill has not had any action on the company ops. We've been to this op area many times before and are probably going back because a new IV Corps commander is arriving.

Tom and I are trying to keep our spirits high by designing a "Swamp Rat" patch and making up some by-laws for membership! (*Unfortunately, I was not able to find any trace of the patch or by-laws among my letters to Pat.*)

3 JUL 68

I'm back from our battalion operation. We swam more than we walked. The skies opened up this morning, and it is still raining. I've changed to my one pair of dry shorts and am in my hammock shielded from the rain by my poncho. It doesn't take much anymore to make me happy since we are so miserable on these operations.

We had an interesting meal today. It was served in a pretty bowl and was full of funny-looking stuff oozing a bright red liquid. I'm pretty sure it was ground-up entrails mixed with peanuts. It was a little too much for Bill, who needed to excuse himself halfway through the first bowl. Since the Vietnamese were snickering, I covered for him by having a second helping! This was followed by a traditional 15-day old duck egg. They aren't too bad as long as I don't look at an eyeball and spit out any feathers!

Interestingly enough, I seem to be getting along with my counterpart and everyone else better than ever. I'm surprised since I seem to be one of the few advisors who is willing to say no to my counterpart's request when I believe the Vietnamese should make their own system work.

I just heard that Maj Joe Loughlin, another classmate from our AWS class, was killed last month up in I Corps. We are losing some mighty fine Marines in this war. I'm embarrassed now and feel guilty to think back to my time at Quantico, when I was hoping the war would last long enough for me to get over here . . . and yet I'm sure I'll feel the same way about the next one. How else could a Marine feel?

In fact, when the Gulf War began, I had recently turned over command of the 4th MEB (Marine Expeditionary Brigade) at Camp Pendleton, CA, been promoted to Major General, and begun serving as the Combined/Joint staff officer for plans, policy, and strategy for the US Forces in Korea. The 4th MEB was committed and landed in Kuwait. I did feel guilty that I was not able to be with them.

Happy birthday to young Bill.

5 JUL 68

Bill slipped into Cần Thơ' yesterday and brought back some mail. Yeaaaa! And with our ponchos hanging up to keep us dry, I am trying to catch up on answering those letters.

We will be conducting company-size ops tomorrow. About all we seem to be finding lately are a few weapons, ammunition caches, and booby traps . . . which occasionally result in casualties.

6 JUL 68

My counterpart drove to Task Force Hq today but I stayed back. As a result, our mail from Sài gòn was not picked up. I won't make that mistake again. You would think that TF Hq would make more of an effort to support us . . . in between taking their hot showers, eating at the Army mess hall, and visiting the post exchange and club! Do I sound a little bitter? Don't worry, I'm only spouting off to you. I'm still fine. It will not affect my job.

Tom moved out on a 5th Battalion operation this afternoon and Bill moved back to our last location with one of our companies, to be in reserve in case there is heavy enemy contact.

8 JUL 68

The 5th Battalion had heavy contact yesterday and had quite a few casualties. We are leaving now to go help.

Happy anniversary!

11 JUL 68

You won't believe it. I still don't. The next morning after I last wrote, our 4th Battalion left the outskirts of Cần Thơ' by truck at 3:30 am, headed for the river, and boarded the boats of a Vietnamese RAG (River Assault Group). The senior advisor had been in the 14th Company with me at USNA, class of '61. I remembered him well.

We went ashore at 7:30 am and spent the rest of the day wading and swimming, trying to link up with the 3rd Battalion. We stopped only once for a short noon chow break. By dark, we were receiving orders faster than we could react . . . extract, don't extract, go by boat, go by helo, walk . . . so we continued to plod. Fortunately, we had no enemy contact that day because we were vulnerable, but a Vietnamese Ranger battalion to our south stumbled into a VC platoon and was able to call in a pair of helo gunships, which took care of the situation.

Meanwhile, we staggered on. One of our Marines fell into a ravine and I found him face down and buried up to his waist in mud. It took me 15 minutes to pull him out and get him moving again. Everyone was mentally and physically exhausted from the last two-and-a-half months of this foolishness. As if that wasn't enough, about 9 pm, an Army helo gunship, who had been supporting Tom and the 3rd Battalion, suddenly opened fire on us, the 3rd Battalion, and the Rangers who were closing on us! Miraculously, only one man was hit. He died yesterday . . . another casualty of friendly fire. (*We had way too many of these useless deaths.*) Overall, we had 11 WIAs, one KIA, and we found several VC weapons with four VC KIAs.

We were finally extracted by boat and arrived back at Cần Thơ at 3:30 am only to find more confusion on where to bed down and spend the night. TF Hq personnel were not back from the operation, so Bill and I used their command post for the rest of the night. Bill was in bad shape with cramps and chills. He's better now, but I've got the runs again and am trying to control it with pills.

Yesterday was spent in the pouring-down rain waiting for a decision to return to our base camp. Our TF Commander has requested that our MAU Hq do something to get us out of here. I've eaten two mess-hall meals since we arrived back here and felt sick after each one. Back to Vietnamese food for me. Tom's assistant advisor has the same symptoms as Bill.

We are finally settled in a small partially destroyed villa just outside town. It has a roof, walls, and a tile floor. I have no idea how long we will stay here, but for now, I'm dry.

15 JUL 68

We went back out into the muck with the 3rd Battalion and the Rangers again. It was a long three days but we are back in Cần Thơ. Being able to have a hot shower and a cold drink is almost an indescribable event. I went two days without water this time. Still no word from Sài gòn on when or if we will ever leave here. Our troops are in bad shape. Tom's 3rd Battalion is worse off and has almost 60% with trench foot, intestinal sickness, or both. Both of our assistants have pretty bad feet right now. I take my boots off at least once a day, squeeze out my socks, and massage my feet. They look like sponges! Tom and I are still doing fine and somehow keep plodding along.

We had repeated VC contacts on this op but were not allowed to pursue. It was only sniper fire and a few B-40 rockets, but each time we were ordered to stop by TF Hq, according to Maj Vuong.

Not sure why. Maybe higher Hq doesn't trust my counterpart to keep us from walking into a trap. On one occasion, when our CP group was sprayed with automatic weapons fire from a sniper, he disappeared, and it took me several minutes to find him . . . down in a bunker to the rear of us. I tried to get him to come out and move forward with me to call in fire support on the sniper, but he wouldn't move. I then talked a company commander into moving forward with me, but by then, the sniper was gone. Maj Vuong wants me to call for helo gunships anytime we hear enemy fire. He won't move forward without them. I've stopped doing that unless the threat is more than I believe our battalion can handle on its own. We have already had two helos hit by VC ground fire on this op, but both made it back okay.

Amazingly, I still seem to be getting along very well with all the Vietnamese. This morning Maj Vuong presented me with a brand new tiger suit, compliments of the battalion. I guess I embarrassed them walking around in my shorts!

We are scheduled to stay here in Cần Thơ for a few days while the 3rd Battalion goes on an op, and then we will flip flop. We can use a few days to rest.

I know I gripe a lot in my letters, but my attitude and performance are not suffering. The letters are just my way of letting off steam. These young Marine officers and enlisted men are good people. They just have a battalion commander with poor leadership skills. There is also some deadwood on the TF Hq staff. It's hard for me to accept the fact that I won't be able to fix it before I rotate to Thailand. The whole Vietnamese command structure is a complex system, and I think that many US advisors find it easier to just go along rather than try to change it. My experiences are still invaluable and I am learning a lot more than I ever expected about people and warfighting. One thing is for sure, the only way to find out what this war is all about is to get down to the Vietnamese level . . . outside of the US compounds!

Enough for today. I feel better now.

16 JUL 68

Believe it or not, we and the 3rd Battalion are still in Cần Thơ. We are being held in reserve, much as we were when we first arrived down here.

This morning, as I stopped by TF Hq, one of the TF Commander's cowboys shot the S-2 (Intelligence Officer), shot another soldier trying to stop him, and then ran into town and blew his brains out! I'm told this happened because another cowboy was being punished unjustifiably. Now that cowboy is threatening suicide. As you can read, the stress and strain of the last two months down here are starting to show. One Marine in Tom's battalion shot himself in the foot this morning so he could go back home.

17 JUL 68

Called Sài gòn today and found out that Col Michael has orders to be a regimental commander up north, and Col Corbett is taking over as the Senior MAU Advisor. The summer rotation of personnel is underway. I'll be on the tail end of that when I leave for Thailand.

We are in reserve while the 3rd Battalion is on an op today.

19 JUL 68

We went on a short op yesterday with helo lifts to and from. All went well, but all we found was a small ammo cache.

This morning Bill went to the Army dispensary and was diagnosed with hepatitis. He will be medevaced back to Sài gòn this afternoon. Tom's assistant has such bad feet from being wet so long that he hasn't been able to walk for several days. Meanwhile Tom and I continue to plug along. Sài gòn has sent another advisor down to fill in with Tom and me on our operations.

20 JUL 68

Went on a short op today . . . just a walk in the sun. It only rained on us once, and we only needed to cross one large rice paddy. It was almost pleasant for a change. The women in the village were weaving straw mats. It was nice to be out of the jungle and see villagers again.

21 JUL 68

Looks like we will go back to Sài gòn on the 25th. TF A with two Battalions will replace us. It's none too soon. Tom's assistant was medevaced today with bad feet, parasites, and extreme dehydration. He looks like a walking ghost, and Tom and I keep plodding along.

22 JUL 68

No activity today. Everyone is still trying to recuperate before we head back to Sài gòn. The Ranger battalions are starting to have the same foot problems we have been suffering. IV Corp Hq has finally caught on that we are all down to less than 50 percent effective strength, and that includes the US advisors! What an experience in wet jungle survival this has been.

The other day, our Vietnamese doctor cut out a small metal fragment from my nose that had started to bother me. I'm pretty sure it's from our Tết battle and it took this long to work up to the skin surface.

I went to church yesterday and it felt good. The sermon was about making the most of what you have. Very appropriate.

24 JUL 68

Well, we went on another operation yesterday. I hope that will be the last time that I have to stay wet all day. Tomorrow, TF B Hq and the 3rd Battalion head back to Sài gòn by truck convoy. We should follow the next day.

This morning our TF advisor, Maj McKinstry went to the dispensary. He is dehydrated and has a bad case of diarrhea. So we have now lost half of our advisors that arrived down here two months ago. (*By the end of my tour, I would have had ten different assistant advisors work for me!*)

25 JUL 68

The TF B Hq and 3rd Battalion are on the way back. I am packed and ready to leave in the morning.

11

27 JUL 68—*written from Sài gòn*

We arrived back in Sài gòn yesterday evening. I'm sitting on the same porch where I used to visit with Gene when we were last here. I've been assigned another assistant advisor until Bill gets well. First Lieutenant Frank Jordan was one of my students at TBS. Big surprise, right?

Tomorrow I will start coordinating everything for our mission here, which is providing security for the CMD. It seems to be much better organized now than our last time here. We will soon see.

28 JUL 68

We just had a wind and rain storm while I was away from my cot on the porch. My poncho was blown away, and no one was around, so everything I have is soaked. I had just picked up the mail, so I will need to let the letters dry before I can read them, and I thought I was through for a while with having everything soaked!

29 JUL 68

I'm staying busy. Frank went on a small company op this morning and I tried to dry out letters and pictures from yesterday. This afternoon Frank and I went to Cat Lái to coordinate an op with the US Army.

I've moved into what looks like a small schoolhouse in order to stay dry. Unfortunately, there are some young Marines in here too . . .

and they have found a guitar and an old songbook. I can barely get my thoughts together as they play and sing. I may not stay in here long!

31 JUL 68

Yesterday I went into the MAU and talked with LtCol Breckinridge. Col Corbett had gone to Vũng Tàu to visit Bill in the hospital. Later I went on a helo reconnaissance of the area with Maj Vuong and we had to make an emergency landing (*in a rice paddy due to engine failure*). However, a medevac helo responded immediately, picked us up, and we were able to finish the recon. It was exciting for a while.

Nothing much happened on our op this morning except that I had to medevac Frank! What a shame. He couldn't keep up and was near collapse. The Vietnamese took notice, of course, so I'll never be able to use him again. We were crossing similar terrain to that in the Delta without as much mud, but lots of water. We had to swim two rivers, but they were easier than down south. I now have another replacement for Bill, Capt Jack Sheehan. (*Jack would do well and years later would retire as a four-star general.*)

General Chapman, our new CMC (Commandant of the Marine Corps), will visit us this weekend. I guess we will all be spit and polish for a change.

1 AUG 68

I met Col Corbett today and look forward to working for him. I've heard many good things about him. We discussed what happened with Frank, and he supported my recommendation of no more duty in the field. Frank is a communications officer and should stay in town in an academic role. I talked with Frank later and explained my position to him in a cordial way. I think he understood.

The MAU operations officer, who is a supply officer by background, somehow managed, without notifying me, to set up a 106mm recoilless rifle class for our Vietnamese Marines to switch them over from our smaller, lighter 57mm recoilless rifles. (Partly based on my recommendations after our Huế Citadel battle.) It will require adding eight more Jeeps per battalion to mount and carry the heavier RRs plus the ammo. I found out when an Hq crew showed up unannounced this morning to start doing familiarization firing, so I sent them back. This was the second item I discussed at MAU Hq with the colonel! These kinds of things need to be coordinated ahead of time!

On the lighter side, I managed to have my hair cut for the CMC visit and found out that I may have an opportunity to visit Bangkok in September to find out more about my new job!

2 AUG 68

I had an enjoyable visit with Col Corbett this morning and discussed a growing concern we are having with local militia and US forces firing their weapons as they highballed down the highway through our positions. I will try to coordinate with the Army colonel at Cát Lái

We have a small op scheduled for tomorrow, which Jack is anxious to go on.

It is really nice to be able to receive mail on a regular basis again.

4 AUG 68

Just returned from church. Yesterday was busy all day. It started at about 4 am, when a helo gunship crash landed about a mile from here. The CMD wanted a US presence to stay with the helo until daylight after the pilot and crew were medevaced. My driver and I headed that way and found the helo not far from the highway. I stayed there until I was relieved about 8:30 am. Jack and our small op started at 6 am, and I was a little concerned about monitoring them in case of a problem, but it worked out.

Later Jack and I visited Cát Lái and talked with the Army colonel there about the indiscriminate firing of weapons in our area. Not sure it will help the situation, but we tried. On the way back, we looked at all of our defensive positions along the road and put together some recommendations for improved security. I couldn't find Maj Vuong but will offer my thoughts to him and TF Hq when

I see them. There is much room for improvement. But all I can do is offer advice and be patient.

This evening, CMC talked to all US Marines in Sài gòn. He will visit our MAU Hq tomorrow. I saw several old friends while at the CMC talk. TF is sending a replacement to monitor my radio tomorrow during our op so I can be there to meet CMC.

We are having the daily monsoon showers here, but not nearly as bad as in the Delta. The good news is that it cools down in the evening and makes it easier to sleep.

I am much busier up here with reports and coordination than I was in the Delta.

5 AUG 68

Met Gen Chapman this morning at MAU Hq and he awarded medals to several of us. Afterward, he made us all feel very proud with his comments.

7 AUG 68

My orders finally arrived for the tour in Bangkok. Time to start thinking about moving, passports, and shots. October is just around the corner. I'll be able to get back to Woodbridge in time to turn around and head back this way!

10 AUG 68

The rain continues, and I'm feeling a little damp. I've just returned from inspecting the Newport bridge we are responsible for defending. It is on the east entrance to Sài gòn. Our Marines were more alert than the last time I checked on them but still leave a lot to be desired. My talk with Maj Vuong must have had some impact. I've asked Col Corbett to come visit tomorrow and see what I've been complaining about. There has been little progress made in improving the bridge defense since we were last here before going down to the Delta. I'm hoping we can make some progress in having the Vietnamese correct the situation. Jack has been pulled back to the MAU and another assistant has been sent to me.

11 AUG 68

I'm starting to feel like our advisory effort might have an impact after all. I'll either be relieved or looked upon as a different way of doing things when this is over relative to the Newport Bridge issue. The 4th Battalion has been responsible for the bridge security for three days now, and I have made recommendations on how to make improvements to Maj Vuong each day. He had not responded until today after he found out Col Corbett had visited with me and agreed with me on the security. It could also be pressure from the TF commander, whom I've kept informed.

At any rate, by noon today, my counterpart was running scared and confronted me about the bridge security situation. I explained the role of the advisor and my responsibilities to him, and emphasized how long the Vietnamese have been in charge of bridge security with very little being done to improve the situation. I showed him my several pages of recommended corrections. He was quite upset that he might be ordered to carry out these recommendations. But we talked it through, and I think everything is fine for now.

This afternoon, BGen Eshenberg, an Army one-star general who works for Gen Abrams showed up and he also agreed with all my recommendations. However, I tried to emphasize that unless the orders to improve security are reinforced down the Vietnamese chain of command, we are not doing our job of advising properly. The general informed me that Gen Abrams had relieved several advisors for not getting the job done. I held my ground and reiterated that we should try to make the Vietnamese chain of command work and not give in and do everything for them. He then listened to me for another hour and forty-five minutes! Another temporary assistant for me, Maj Carter Swenson, had just arrived and got quite an earful. We had a few laughs after the general left. Not sure what the other advisors up here are thinking about the ruckus I'm causing, but Col Corbett hasn't fired me yet.

12 AUG 68

The Army general who visited yesterday had the US Army Big Red One Division deliver 6000 sandbags to us today! So much for making the Vietnamese system work. But Col Corbett scolded his counterpart Col Laan, Chief of Staff, VNMC, today, who then called all the battalion commanders together for a talk. I'm finally getting support from the top down.

13 AUG 68

Nothing spectacular happened today. I drove into Sài gòn and had a nice chat with Col Corbett. He complimented me and said he would back us all the way in trying to make the advisor system work. Unfortunately, a senior Army general visited another bridge today, the Newport, which is defended by another VNMC battalion with a new, inexperienced advisor. The general's parting comment to our advisor was that "If this bridge is blown up, it will all rest on your shoulders!" I wish he had come to our bridge and said that. The poor Army command structure seems to have no idea of how to deal with the Vietnamese. The Army senior officers are putting the burden on their advisors in the field without providing any support by telling their own counterparts what needs to be done. How sad.

Maj Vuong and I walked through the bridge defenses today, and he finally told me he didn't know how to fix it. I showed him, and this afternoon our Marines started filling sandbags and building bunkers! I found out later that he had complained to Col Laan and the TF Commander about me and they told him that I was doing my job . . . and that he better start doing his!

This morning Maj Vuong took me to breakfast and later today brought me some goodies to eat. Maybe we are starting to see some progress . . . or maybe he is just trying to save his job.

14 AUG 68

Notice the date. Before long this whole tour will only be a memory. Parts of it will be good to remember, but my frustration needs to fade away.

Our little operation today was over by early afternoon and had negative results. Maj Swenson went along as my assistant to observe and learn before he takes over as a battalion senior advisor.

The bridge situation is improving rapidly. Apparently, Maj Vuong is feeling the pressure from above and has conceded to my recommendations. We toured the bridge together today, and he instructed his company commanders exactly as I had explained yesterday. The bunkers are being built, and when I pointed out some mistakes, they concurred and began to correct. Finally, I'm beginning to feel like I'm doing my job. Maj Vuong still has a long way to go, but he is now inspecting the bridge on his own, requesting materials through the Vietnamese system, and instructing his subordinates on what needs to be done.

This may not seem like much as you read, but it was a major accomplishment for me, and a major stepping stone to the accomplishment of the US advisory effort. Without the Vietnamese military stepping up and making their system of support work, I could see no hope for them to win this war. We would not be able to win it for them.

I could very easily coast for the last two months and stay off the skyline, but I can't, and I don't think anyone expects that from me. I'm starting to see results in this battalion and within the rest of the unit as well, so it has been worth all the heartburn.

I'm sure it helped that Col Bùi The Laan, VNMC Chief of Staff, and I were in the same platoon going through TBS as lieutenants in 1959-60.

17 AUG 68

Just when I thought we were making progress, Maj Vuong made a false report on the number of US sandbags received. Additionally, the bunkers are not being built correctly. I continue to explain, but to no avail. I've asked the Brigade Hq to hold up further materials until Maj Vuong requests help in constructing the bunkers. I think he is afraid to ask for help since it might be conceived as a loss of face.

I know I am walking a fine line right now between the Vietnamese thinking that I'm harassing them vs. trying to help them. At this point, in my opinion, about all my counterpart has going for him is his ability to host a good party!

Bill returned from Vũng Tàu yesterday, but now will go on R&R to Taiwan to complete his recovery. He still looks sick to me. My Jeep is also sick, and so it goes in this far off land of my frustration.

My highlight of the day was an unexpected visit by Col Laan and the TF Commander who inspected the bridge with Maj Vuong! There is still hope.

19 AUG 68

I'm spending today at the MAU Hq trying to finish my counterpart evaluation. It is lengthy with much detail and many examples in order to make my point on where I think he can improve on leadership qualities.

21 AUG 68

I love receiving mail on a regular basis.

I have finished the first draft of my counterpart evaluation. I need to talk with Col Corbett before going smooth because it is a derogatory report. I think it will set the stage for Col Laan to remove an unsatisfactory battalion commander who is impeding the progress of the VNMC. Additionally, I hope it will provide a baseline for my replacement to evaluate this battalion.

I will say that the 4th Battalion now has completed building bunkers for the first time in almost the proper positions to defend our bridge . . . and they were built by the Vietnamese with only advisor recommendations at the command level. I'm convinced, as is Col Corbett, that the advisor effort has been misdirected for a long time either by mistake or ignorance. Starting at the top, our senior US commanders have put pressure on their advisors to get the job done regardless of Vietnamese participation. The Vietnamese, as a result, have learned that if they drag their feet long enough, the advisor will use US assets to accomplish the mission while they watch.

A good example is the sandbags for our bridge. The US Army one-star general who visited me and "encouraged" me to go get sandbags for our bunkers, ended up ordering a US Army Division to deliver them to us. This was after I refused to order them myself because the sandbags were available in the Vietnamese system, and I believe that our advisory role is to help them make their system work. If Col Corbett had not supported me, I'm sure I would have been relieved.

Tomorrow I've scheduled a trip to Vũng Tàu to check on our battalion base camp. I've asked Col Corbett to invite Col Laan to come along. This will force my counterpart to go and we will find out what, if anything, has been done to improve his dependent housing area. I know from Bill that nothing has been done since we were last there. You may recall that I had set up a well project for them. This is all about forcing the Vietnamese to use their system of support by going through their chain of command. But the politics at the top are almost more than I can handle.

22 AUG 68

The VC fired 20 rockets into Sài gòn this morning. Everyone scurried around for a while and then it was over, so we are still going to Vũng Tàu today. As I suspected, Maj Vuong was not interested in going until he heard that Col Laan was going. Now he is ready to go.

23 AUG 68

The Vũng Tàu trip was a success. Although Maj V had not done much for his battalion family housing area before we arrived, he now is interested thanks to Col Laan. I re-coordinated the fresh water-well that I had arranged before, but Maj Vuong must formally request it and follow through on where and when it should be dug. I hope we can get this done before I rotate home, or it may never happen.

The other battalions were moved around today, but Maj Vuong was left here with the Newport Bridge and given another one as well. Very interesting! I can see some stress in my counterpart's face.

24 AUG 68

We had a small operation today with no results. Bill is back from Taiwan so the first team is finally back in action. Another US Army general came by to look at our bridge. I asked Maj Vuong to brief him and then pointed out that the Vietnamese were building the defensive structures by themselves with only my advice . . . and I explained why. He agreed. No pressure on me this visit. Another sign that maybe we are progressing in the right direction.

Just heard that two of our advisors were wounded down in the Delta by mortar fire. The war goes on.

25 AUG 68

Our advisors down south were not hurt badly, thank goodness.

Col Corbett has given me the okay to pull Bill and myself from the battalion if my counterpart doesn't support us adequately. He swings back and forth like a yo-yo depending on the pressure from above.

My USMC uniforms that I left in Okinawa never caught up to me here and are presumed lost. I will have to have new ones made.

27 AUG 68

I'm going to Vũng Tàu alone in two days and will try to finish up the projects for our battalion dependents. If the dependents were not so neglected I would not be doing this myself, but I feel obligated and Maj Vuong just can't seem to do much here in Vũng Tàu except party.

We are living under the bridge these days and Maj Vuong has a small room for himself while I'm left out with all the radios. I insisted on some privacy, and he finally gave in. I now have my own small space; another small victory.

A month from tomorrow I leave for a few days in Bangkok in order to check on my new job. I'm counting the days.

29 AUG 68—*written from Vũng Tàu*

I'm writing from my favorite place in Vietnam, the USO in Vũng Tàu. Today I was able to coordinate and process the paperwork for four new wells, a new school house, a playground, and new roofs and improvements for family housing. Not sure how much will be finished before I leave country. I had lunch with the battalion base camp commander and he was grateful for my efforts, not so appreciative of Maj Vuong. I think the word is out that I'm recommending the relief of my counterpart.

30 AUG 68—*written from Sài gòn*

We ran a small op this morning with our Marines in small boats and with Maj Vuong and me in a helo. What a difference from the Delta when we were in the mud and water all day and night.

Bill went into MAU Hq and was awarded a Silver Star for his valor during our Huế battle, and given a regular Marine Corps commission. He is no longer a reserve officer on contract. It was quite a nice morning for him.

That means he didn't have to sign a contract every couple of years to stay on active duty. He could now remain on active duty until he resigns, retires, or is asked to leave.

This afternoon I moved into a room in the Splendid Hotel, where the permanent Sài gòn advisors live. With six weeks to go on my tour, I finally have a place to lay out and sort my gear. It will also be nice to take a hot shower on a regular basis. I'm looking forward to reading a book tonight with an electric light to see!

1 SEP 68

This will probably be my last month with the 4th Battalion. If I fly to Bangkok on the 28th for a few days and my relief has arrived in Sài gòn, there will be little reason for me to return to the battalion.

Tom and I had a long talk with Col Corbett yesterday concerning my after-tour report, which recommends among other things, that my counterpart be relieved of command due to incompetence. It will be shown to Col Laan and Lt Gen Kahn, VNMC Commandant. I am so anxious to finish this tour, and yet I know the job is not finished. It is difficult to look back over my last eleven months in Vietnam and find anything lasting that has been accomplished. I can only hope. The 4th Battalion deserves better, and I hope they will soon have a better leader.

I'm starting to think that it may well be our advisory effort that is prolonging this war and probably making it unwinnable, at least in the short term. MACV does not appear interested in trying to convince the Vietnamese chain of command to issue orders concerning unit support from the top down. Instead, it is much easier for US higher Hq to hold US advisors responsible while the Vietnamese sit back and watch us do our thing. It would seem that the only people who want the war to end are the peasants. The Vietnamese politicians and the upper ranking military officers have never had it better . . . what with payoffs from a thriving black market.

I had heard about the black market before I arrived, but refused to believe it until I saw it for myself. Now I've seen it and believe that we, the US, are at fault. It's not only Vietnamese. I'm told that there are US civilians and ex-military clearing $1,200 to $1,500 per month tax-free. Truckloads of imported goodies disappear from the pier as soon as they are off-loaded and go immediately to the black market. I don't know how to stop it at my level. It can only be dealt with from the top down, and that does not appear likely anytime soon. It's no wonder that some of the Vietnamese leaders do not appear anxious for the war to end.

There! I got that off my chest!

Meanwhile, to make my earlier point, the US Army delivered fifty-six rolls of concertina barbed wire to our bridge yesterday. No one in authority had coordinated with my counterpart and no one from the 4th Battalion was there to accept it. So it sits.

2 SEP 68

Col Corbett stopped by and inspected our bridge today. The bunkers had not been worked on since I stopped putting pressure on Maj Vuong. Col Corbett also noticed a rusty 81mm mortar and no officers around. He is recommending that the mortar be returned to higher HQ if not cleaned up. I am unable to find Maj Vuong right now to discuss this latest issue.

I'm still not bitter, nor do I dislike the Vietnamese. I'm just disappointed that I haven't been able to do more.

3 SEP 68

I have talked with Maj Vuong about Col Corbett's visit yesterday. He was visibly shaken again and immediately started chewing out his subordinates. It will be short-lived. We are forcing them to work on the bridge defenses. They are dragging their feet because another battalion will take over the bridge in a few days . . . and then the new battalion can do the work!

Sometimes I wonder if I'm doing the right thing by making waves? I wonder if anything would ever change if I just played nice guy? With Gene already gone, and Tom and I close to finishing our tour, will there be other advisors willing to continue our cause to help the Vietnamese help themselves?

5 SEP 68

We are in a state of limbo after several changes in our next mission. For a short while, it sounded like we were going to be sent up north. Instead, we are back where we started when we arrived from down in the Delta. A Vietnamese Ranger battalion has taken over the Newport Bridge, and our other two VNMC battalions have been attached to ARVN divisions. It looks like a slow piecemeal dissection of our VNMC to me. It also appears to be very political.

6 SEP 68

I walked out on the battalion and Maj Vuong yesterday evening and took Bill with me. I did not go back to the hotel and am staying at TF Hq so that I can monitor the tactical situation and still help out if there is a problem. I also have asked the nearest other battalion advisor to respond if necessary.

I left because of lack of respect from my counterpart. Yesterday, for the first time, I had to move myself to our new location and then set up my gear since my cowboy, Chiến, had been sent on leave. Maj Vuong never mentioned this to me, nor has he assigned a replacement cowboy. There are many other reasons, some I've written about earlier. I thought we had worked through most of them, but things have deteriorated since I've begun to insist that he use his Vietnamese chain of command before he asks for US support, especially in regard to building bridge defenses.

Fortunately, Col Corbett is backing me 100%. Otherwise, I would have been relieved by now. We have set down some conditions for Maj Vuong, if he would like to talk with me, and a few other conditions, if he wants an advisor back with his battalion. This is unprecedented in their culture, and perhaps for the MAU as well. It will result, I hope, in Maj Vuong being replaced as battalion commander. Although it might seem like a game, I believe that the battalion deserves a leader who is competent.

Tom, who is now the TF advisor, has presented my case to the TF commander. I await the result.

7 SEP 68

I'm back with the battalion. Maj Vuong was ordered to report to the TF commander, and I met with them and Tom there. It was all very professional. I stated why I had left the battalion and that I demanded respect for US Marine officers, and that I refused to have to keep requesting those things essential to our well-being. I took my time and emphasized each point. Maj Vuong accepted my conditions and asked that I return to the battalion. I agreed but stated that if my conditions were not met, I would leave the battalion for good! The meeting lasted about an hour. I did not compromise on any of my demands. I'm guessing Maj Vuong was ordered to accept them, since I'll only be there another three weeks.

As a side note, my new Jeep driver, Nam, whom I have had since our last stay in Vũng Tàu, made a special trip to see me at TF Hq soon after I left the battalion, and tried to talk me into returning. He also worked all last night on my Jeep to fix some problem. He has tried hard to fill in for Chiến and I would love to take him to Bangkok with me!

I'm hoping everything will go smoothly now and my replacement will either have a new battalion commander or at least, the ground rules should be clear.

8 SEP 68

Today was a beautiful day. I went to church. Maj Vuong is being extra nice to me, but I'm not seeing any improvement in the battalion. However, there is progress in Vũng Tàu on constructing the wells for the battalion dependents.

Our battalion moved further east toward Long Bình this afternoon, but now it sounds like we will fly west tomorrow toward Tây Ninh. Something is going on there.

12

We did fly out of Sài gòn and now are located SE of Tây Ninh near the Michelin rubber plantation. B-52 strikes have been dropping bombs continuously for some time. Intelligence reports indicate that there is enemy activity close by. The Cambodian border is about twelve miles to the west. This country is different from everywhere else I've been in that the forests are unbelievable. You could hide an entire division in here . . . about 25,000 men. As we flew in by helicopter yesterday, I was able to have a pretty good look at the area. I'll spend most of today trying to coordinate with the other units already here. There is plenty of support if I can figure out the command relationships. Maj Voung has escaped the pressures of Sài gòn, but it remains to be seen how he will handle this new situation.

The Vietnamese seem to think that all the VNMC battalions have been sent away from Sài gòn so that their Commandant, LtGen Khan, can be relieved of command without incident. Always politics! But it's starting to feel like we might also be in on the beginning of another big battle. This whole area is a staging ground for the NVA coming across from Cambodia.

There is a US Army advisory team located here in our village. They, of course, have set up their own separate quarters with hot showers, TV, stereo, movies, US chow, etc. Maybe they have the right idea. I don't know anymore. I am glad, though, that I was able to try our concept of advising first.

I'm in a lovely little home owned by a village official. He and his family treat us with respect, and I can speak just enough Vietnamese to have fun with them. Their meals are excellent. They sleep several in a hard raised bed and think nothing of it. All eight kids have left for school, which is here in the village. It was not attacked during Tết, although there has been a lot of action just up the road in Tây Ninh, as well as over in the Michelin plantation.

14 SEP 68—*written from Tây Ninh*

I've been in Tây Ninh for the last three days. We joined a US Army Airborne brigade in the pouring-down rain early on the 12th and were ordered to attack immediately. It was not a very good situation. Maj Voung is not the most aggressive guy in the world and we had a lot of foot dragging. It was a night attack, which is not easy, but I had plenty of fire support standing by to make it work. We made enemy contact at first light. Bill stayed with the lead company and fought until dark while I coordinated all the fire support.

We lost 12 KIA and 27 WIA the first two days. We found several weapons and NVA bodies but they had carried or dragged off many more. At 2:15 am on the 13th we started receiving friendly artillery fire. No one was hurt, and it finally ended about 2:50 am. I never found out who was firing at us or why!

At one point I had problems getting helo gunship support, but we finally worked it out. During this time I had more reporters and newsmen with me than I ever did at Huế . . . about 25! John Wheeler from UPI released some of his observations prematurely, which then caused Gen Abrams to send Col Corbett up by private helo to see me and check on the accuracy of the UPI report! I confirmed the report and hope that helps open some minds in Sài gòn as to what is really happening here in this war.

I had several "higher ups" flying in to talk with me. I found out later that Pat read about me in the Washington Post the next day! The essence of it was that we were in contact with the enemy and trying to rescue a wounded Marine. I had requested helo gunship support to cover a rescue team, and the adjacent US Army unit in charge of the helos told me they had other priorities. I told them mine were pretty high on the list and they essentially told me the

Vietnamese were not priority. The press was right there overhearing the radio conversation and immediately began to interview me. I simply said Marines didn't leave their own behind. We would rescue our wounded and dead . . . and we did. The article made the Army look pretty bad, but was in fact accurate . . . and Washington was on the phone to Gen Abrams immediately! Somehow I survived once more! But unfortunately, I heard that an Army officer was relieved for making the Army look bad in the press.

Things have slowed down a bit now. An Airborne battalion was dropped in close by yesterday and has already lost twice as many men as we have on this operation. Another Airborne battalion is being dropped in now. We have two of our companies chasing the NVA northwest of town but lost contact with them yesterday. We are very close to the Cambodian border, and I suspect the NVA were trying to move supplies closer to their units in Sài gòn when we found them.

We've had a Filipino Civic Action Group following us since yesterday, clearing roads, feeding civilians, and offering medical aid. This is good because we caused about as much damage in town here as we did in Huế. Not pretty! But this time, most of the civilians were able to leave before we destroyed their town.

Interesting that the newspaper reports that Pat sent me about this battle downplayed what really happened. We did a lot of damage in town, had some serious firefights, killed a lot of enemy, and suffered a lot of losses.

Don't know how much longer we will be here or when we will see another Marine unit.

17 SEP 68

All is quiet today in Tây Ninh. Looks like their biggest attack was in our direction. We pushed them south and then blocked as the Airborne battalion wiped them out. It was a pretty good operation after we finally got it coordinated. Right now we have two companies sweeping the area to make sure it's secure.

The Airborne forces will leave today and then we will be working with the Popular and Regional Forces, who are the local Vietnamese militia.

18 SEP 68

Nothing happening today. We're still in Tây Ninh. We are working out of the local Province headquarters. I would rather be back out in the field. The local Province Chief, our new boss, has caused us to spread each of our companies into a different area. Our battalion now stretches from one end of town to the other. We expect the VC to mount an attack sometime soon, but who knows for sure?

I've been trying to convince the Army advisors at Sector, Province, and Corps level to plan another operation while we still have the enemy on its heels . . . and then have the order come down from the ARVN Corps Commander to our battalion. That's what it will take to get my counterpart to do anything other than just sit here.

No mail since moving up here. I'm becoming very frustrated again.

19 SEP 68

Now I'm really disgusted. Our chain of command has been made clear. We don't do anything unless the III Corps Commander approves . . . and he has us essentially sitting here in a perimeter around Tây Ninh.

In the area where we had been, there was some more serious action yesterday. Three of our Marine advisors were wounded. Both Tom's and one of my former assistant advisors were shot and are in critical condition. Another of my former assistants was also hurt, but I'm not sure how bad. We are down to only one advisor in each of several battalions. We need more advisors to fill in. I guess the Marine Corps didn't plan on so many of us being wounded this year.

It has continued to rain most of the time we've been here. I guess I'm not going to get out of the monsoon season until my tour is over next month.

14

It seems like we have had at least 100 changes in orders from higher Hq since I last wrote from Tây Ninh. However, we arrived back in Sài gòn last night and then headed to Vũng Tàu this morning.

I talked with Col Corbett for a half hour last night and found out that two of our wounded advisors have been medevaced to Japan. He also told me that my counterpart is being investigated by the Joint General Staff in Sài gòn, based on a formal complaint from the III Corps Commander, recommending that Maj Voung be relieved of command based on his lack of action in Tây Ninh (and probably my constant prodding to higher headquarters to send us on another operation). Col Corbett said he provided my written assessments of Maj Vuong over the last few months to the Joint General Staff to back up the recommendation. The best part is that this is now a Vietnamese initiative and will be a Vietnamese decision.

At one point a few days ago, while still in Tây Ninh, we were ordered to fly over to the Cambodian border and protect an ARVN outpost that had been recently overrun, but was being rebuilt. I was unable to talk Maj Vuong into moving. He kept calling folks and complaining about the command relationships until our mission was canceled. I think this action alone could have triggered the Corps Commander investigation.

It was so good to arrive back in Vũng Tàu, take a hot shower, and get clean last night. Bill and I then went for a walk on the beach and around town talking with some of the people. I really enjoy that. It's the best part of a long, challenging year.

The battalion is scheduled to go back down to the Delta on the 25th. I'm supposed to fly to Bangkok to coordinate on my new job about the same time. I've offered to cancel that and stay here with the battalion since we are short on advisors right now. Col Corbett said no, I will go to Bangkok!

22 SEP 68

Col Corbett called and said that a Joint General Staff team will be here tomorrow to talk with Maj Vuong, who has submitted his request to be relieved. Wow! Can you believe it? Not sure whether he volunteered due to pressure or was told to do it. Either way, mission accomplished! I have no idea who the new commander will be or who will relieve me, but I'm sure Maj Vuong's relief won't take place until after I'm gone. There needs to be some face-saving.

24 SEP 68

Yesterday the JGS team talked with Maj Vuong and then me. They seemed to appreciate my viewpoint but had nothing to say about the Vietnamese decision on Maj Vuong. The battalion will go back to Sài gòn tomorrow and then head for Cần Thơ on the 26th. Still don't know if I'll be going with them. I'll be glad to talk with Col Corbett tomorrow and find out what's going on.

I continue to coordinate with CORDS on the well and other projects for our battalion dependents. There has been no work done on the wells to date. CORDS is waiting for the VNMC to show some interest. I picked up some money from CORDS to buy materials and gave it to Maj Vuong. I explained again that the US will help, but the Vietnamese have to show some interest! I would not be pushing this project if not for my concern for the poor Marine dependents.

You may be wondering what the present relationship is between my counterpart and me. It is surprisingly good, considering all that is going on. In fact, he has been nicer of late than ever before. How could he not know that I've been the source of most of the recent pressure on him? I'm completely in the dark.

25 SEP 68—*written from Sài gòn*

I have officially left the battalion as of today! Bill went down by convoy with the battalion to Cần Thơ today. I flew down later by helo with Col Corbett and briefed Capt Tom Taylor, who shifted over from the 5th Battalion to become my replacement. I'm back in Sài gòn now and will leave for Bangkok on the 28th.

Maj Vuong's relief is still up in the air but appears imminent. It seems to be a question of whether he will be fired or allowed to request relief. I missed my battalion going-away party in Vũng Tàu and did not have a chance to say good bye formally like I had planned, since the decision on my relief wasn't made until last night. I asked Bill to present my gifts to Maj Vuong. He did, and they gave me a nice plaque in return.

I'll try to finish my after-action report on the Tây Ninh operation before leaving for Bangkok, and then start my after-tour report when I return.

28 SEP 68

I'm sitting at the Tân Sơn Nhứt airfield waiting for my plane to Bangkok. Tom is going with me. Col Corbett decided we both needed a break! It will be more fun for me to have Tom along. We should be back by 3 Oct, and I'll head back to the states around 12 Oct. Hard to believe this tour is almost over.

4 OCT 68

Returned from Bangkok yesterday. Spent today talking with Col Corbett and working on my after-tour report. Tom has become very bitter over the Vietnamese command structure and the way it operates, much as Gene had become before he left Vietnam. I'm still trying to remain objective, but as I've written earlier, it has been a struggle for me as well. I'm certainly not bitter, but I am so much better informed now than I was before the Tết offensive.

6 OCT 68

Need to alert you to a new wound I incurred from my trip to Bangkok. Walking back to the hotel after visiting the headquarters where I'll be working, I cut through an alley and hit my head trying to duck under a concrete archway. It bled enough that I headed for the hospital and had it sewed up. I'm a little embarrassed. No Purple Heart this time!

7 OCT 68

The two advisors who were seriously wounded have been evacuated back to the US and will be laid up from six to 12 months. The others that have been hurt are back on their feet and in the field again. We are starting to get new advisors in daily now. Where have they been?

I wrote most of my after-tour report last night. I have enjoyed working for Col Corbett. I can't remember ever working for anyone who was as good.

8 OCT 68 —*Last letter*

I'll try one more letter before I leave. I'm still not sure exactly when that will be, but I need to be in Đà nẵng before the 12th. In the meantime, I'm acting as a troubleshooter for Col Corbett. I'll fly out to a couple of the battalions tomorrow to check on some things. I need to finish up some reports, and that should do it for this tour. Can't believe it is all but over!

But it was.

EPILOGUE

PART ONE—I flew to Đà nẵng on Oct 11th and left Vietnam the next morning. That last night in country was spent with a few Air Force pilots, who adopted me for the evening. They hosted me at the Red Dog Saloon, which was their Officers' Club, and put me up for the night in an air-conditioned trailer. What a contrast with my first night in Đà nẵng the year before! Since my orders transferred me from Vietnam directly to Thailand, I was essentially hitchhiking home on military planes so that I could accompany my family from Virginia to Thailand. The first leg was only from Đà nẵng to Guam, but the pilot had called ahead, and they held up a plane on the runway for me that was headed to San Francisco. From there, I bought a commercial ticket to Washington, DC, and landed at Dulles International Airport. I was finally home, but only for a few days. Pat already had buyers for the house, the boat, and the car. The movers were scheduled in a few days, and we would be off for another new adventure. It would be a completely new world for my family, but familiar surroundings for me, albeit much more comfortable and secure! I did visit my monitor at Headquarters Marine Corps before we left for Thailand and asked if he could issue me a set of Temporary Duty Orders to cover the cost of my commercial trip home. His answer was "Do you want the orders to Thailand or not?"

I really didn't have much time to think about the war once I arrived back home. It was more important to get to know my family again and to try and prepare them for a different country . . . different people, different language, different weather, different customs, etc. And then there was the challenge of trying to manage three small children and baggage on and off airplanes for 24 hours through 12 time zones . . . but it was all worth it just to be back with them again.

I don't know how long it took for me to really try and digest what I had experienced in Vietnam. Since USMACTHAI was the back-up headquarters for USMACV in Sài gòn, I was almost immediately reimmersed in what was going on in Vietnam as soon as we arrived in Bangkok. Additionally, because of my job, I was flying back and forth to Sài gòn almost monthly to coordinate between our two commands. I don't think I thought deeply about my own experiences in 1967 and 1968 until we returned to Washington two years later near the end of 1970. It was then that I saw and felt for the first time the strong anti-war feelings. I had missed the RFK and MLK assasinations and those early strong protest marches. I was surprised how strongly some of my non-military friends felt against the war. It was hard to discuss with them. I was wondering when I would be going back for a second tour, and they thought I was crazy.

As it turned out, they had a lot more information about the politics of the war that I didn't begin to absorb until much later. In fact I'm still learning about the decisions that were made back in Washington and how they were made. We didn't have the luxury in those days to sit back after the six o'clock news each evening and discuss the pros and cons of how the Cold War, communism, and the domino theory affected our national policy and strategy of fighting in South East Asia. We were either training for combat or we were actually fighting most of that time. But most of us, I think, certainly went willingly, and would have felt guilty had we not gone.

PART TWO—I found myself back in Huế in October 1972. I had flown in from the USS New Orleans, a helicopter aircraft carrier (LPH), where I was part of the 31st Marine Amphibious Unit Hq as the Intelligence Officer. We were in support of the current Marine advisors and the Vietnamese Marines, with whom I had served in 1967 and 1968. Col, now MGen, Laan was there and asked me about my time in Thailand. It was good to see him again. I was pleased to find out that my old counterpart, Maj Vuong, had been transferred to the ARVN. The advisors were some of the last US military left in-country as the US began its drawdown of our military forces. The US and SVN had agreed during the Paris peace talks with NVN to begin this US drawdown, to allow all Vietnamese military units from both sides to remain in place and observe a ceasefire, that the US would clear all mines from blocking NVN harbors, and that NVN would then release our POWs. We had been clearing the mines by dragging sleds through the water with helicopters for the past month. South Vietnamese President Thieu only agreed to these terms, which clearly favored NVN, after President Nixon agreed to provide fire support and materials to SVN if they were attacked by NVN.

I walked through Hue Citadel as many memories flashed by. I was glad to see the city thriving again. Much of the heavy destruction was still evident . . . the wall could never be completely repaired, but most of the homes had been fixed up and were full of family activities.

On 23 November, Thanksgiving, 1972, I spent the night in Đà nẵng. For a full five minutes, I stood on the edge of the runway and took pictures. There was absolutely no activity! It was hard to believe it was so quiet, having been there when it was in full swing. That evening I stopped by the Red Dog Saloon and saw, much to my surprise, a hand-written message from Jim Roy a Woodbridge, VA, neighbor! He was a Navy pilot flying off of one of the aircraft carriers stationed in the area. We never did connect while we were both overseas, but had much to talk about when we returned home.

On the morning of 4 March 1973, I walked out on the deck of the USS Cleveland and looked out over Hải Phòng harbor, North Vietnam. I felt like we were part of an eerie movie. It was foggy and dreary with gigantic rock formations coming up out of the sea all around us. The water was as smooth as glass, and we could see fish swimming below the surface from time to time. Our POWs in Hanoi were scheduled to be released later that day as part of the Paris Peace Accords. This and other harbors were now clear of the mines that had been dropped earlier to block them from Soviet and Chinese resupply.

Sunset on that day was beautiful. It was red, streaming through the clouds, and bouncing off the glassy sea right into my eyes. It was difficult to watch, but hypnotic as I thought about our POWs being flown out of Hanoi. The harbor was filled with Chinese and NVN junks and fishing boats. The junks with their huge double sails were the prettiest, especially against the sunset. With binoculars, I was able to see right into the little boats, where most of the crews appeared young. The larger junks had mixed crews; perhaps families were aboard. That night it was hard to tell where the stars stopped and the fishing boat lights began. There were lights everywhere. It looked like a thousand little lights trying to make up for the moon. What a strange feeling I had, sitting in the middle of an NVN harbor surrounded by NVN and Chinese small craft fully lit up as if they were ready to take me on the next liberty run ashore.

That would be the end of the war for me, and since I was only halfway through this, my third unaccompanied 12-month overseas tour, I requested R&R, and it was approved. This time I flew all the way home to Virginia and spent five days with my family. I would not see Vietnam again and have not to this day. I have, however, attended several Cố vấn reunions, which included many of those Vietnamese Marines who were able to make their way to the US after the war. The last one was in Houston, where I had the honor of presenting a long overdue Bronze Star medal to my old friend Bùi The Laan for his leadership during the 1972 NVA Easter Offensive. We were both retired major generals by then. Sadly, he passed away a few years later. I had inquired about Maj Vuong at several earlier reunions and was told that he had also made his way to the US and had settled up north somewhere. Bill Fite, my longest-serving assistant advisor, retired as a colonel to south Florida. Col Corbett retired in North Carolina and passed away a few years ago. Gene Gardner also retired as a colonel, and we were able to retell our stories many times as he introduced me to single malt scotch before he succumbed to the effects of Agent Orange. Tom Ward and I served together again before he retired as a lieutenant colonel in eastern Florida. Charlie Davis retired as a lieutenant colonel, and then went on to become a successful businessman, eventually retiring on Hilton Head Island. We, too, have shared many war stories over single malt scotches.

PART THREE—Most of my comments about the war in my letters to Pat referred to "how" I thought we should be fighting, not "if" we should be fighting. I don't recall anyone ever asking us if we wanted to go fight. Just being a Marine answered that question. However, as I became more and more convinced that we were beating ourselves and that political decisions at multiple levels, not our success on the battlefield, was going to determine the outcome, it was hard not to become frustrated.

I liked the Vietnamese people, believed they deserved better . . . and I had high hopes that we could do better for them. I had taken courses on the history of communism and its goals both at the academy and later at TBS. I had been briefed on the "domino theory" and thought I understood it. And it was clear to me that the officers of the TQLC wanted no part of communism. However, it was also clear to me after serving two years in Bangkok that Thailand and the other ASEAN (Association of Southeast Asian Nations) countries (Singapore, the Philippines, Malaysia, and Indonesia) had little interest in communism, even if we let go of South Vietnam. Capitalism was winning in those countries.

So South Vietnam along with Laos and Cambodia was no longer the domino that could cause the rest of Southeast Asia to fall to communism. With the original domino theory no longer valid and a flawed military strategy of body count, restricted bombing in North Vietnam, and a reluctance to teach and allow SVN forces to win the battles, along with a media biased against the war, there was no way for us to stay and win. And with a Paris peace agreement that allowed NVN forces to remain in the south after a ceasefire, and with an American promise to aid and support the SVN forces against any incursion overturned by the Fulbright amendment, there was no way for the SVN forces to win.

Based on several authors that I have read who have done extensive research on the subject, my criticism and thoughts back then don't seem too far off. I'm not sure, however, that any of my recommendations would have made a difference in the long run. The war was always about politics, theirs and ours, not the people and their culture, not the history of the land. It has taken a long time for me to accept that although President Kennedy might have sent US forces there initially for the right foreign policy reason, and although tactically our US forces were able to win almost any battle we chose to engage, things changed under Presidents Johnson and Nixon. The way we were told to fight and the way the results were reported made things worse. The way our most senior leaders ran the war was not only wrong, it made the war unwinnable by the US. We won every battle I fought . . . and it didn't make any difference!

That's not to say that those of us who went and fought did not fight and die honorably. I believe that most of us did what we were told to the best of our ability. We didn't choose that war, but we did choose to serve our country. Wars will always be terrible, and only those who were there will ever know how terrible. That's another part of the problem.

If there is any good news, it's that some of our present-day leaders have been able to understand the lessons learned from our time in Vietnam and apply them to the new war against terrorism. Hopefully. . .

ACKNOWLEDGMENTS

Of course, none of this book could have been written without the letters that Pat saved and the encouragement and help that I received from my son Bill and my daughters Carolyn and Cathy. Additionally, over the many years after the war, I received continual prodding from my good friend Gene to capture some of the history of the VNMC during the 1968 Tết Offensive. I regret that it was not accomplished before his death, but hope that he would have approved of Letters to Pat.

There have been many others along the way that have provided additional encouragement such as my friends from the "Creek"— Mary Ann and Johnny Schaff, Julie Litzinger and Kathryn Parks, and Edna Trimble and Joan DiJoseph, to name a few. And there have been many friends who have read and offered wise counsel on how I might improve the book like Jacqui Widener, Charlie and Claire Davis, Phyllis Gardner, and Shirley Sanders.

Finally, I can't thank my good neighbor Dana Cook enough for the time and effort she spent proofing each page and the advice she offered on how to make the book more readable.

GLOSSARY

A/N—Army/Navy
AMMO—Ammunition
AFB—Air Force Base
ARVN—Army of the Republic of Vietnam
AWS—Amphibious Warfare School, Quantico, VA
BOQ—Bachelor officers' quarters
CAP—Civic Action Platoons
CMC—Commandant of the Marine Corps
CMD—Command Military District, Sài gòn, SVN
COC—Combat operations center
COLA—Cost-of-living allowance
CORDS—Civil Operations and Revolutionary Development Support
Cô Vân—VNMC term for an advisor
CP—Command post
C-RATIONS—Combat rations
DMZ—Demilitarized zone
FAC—Forward air controller
HELO—Helicopter
HOOCH—Small homemade shelter
HQ—Headquarters
KIA—Killed in action
LDO—Limited duty officer
LZ—Landing zone
MACV—Military Assistance Command, Vietnam
MACTHAI—Military Assistance Command, Thailand
MAF—Marine Amphibious Force

MARS—Military auxiliary radio system
MATA—Military Assistance Training for Advisors, Ft Bragg, NC
MAU—Marine Advisory Unit
MAU—Marine Amphibious Unit
NCO—Non-commissioned officer
NLF—National Liberation Front
NVA—North Vietnamese Army
OP—Operation
PF—Provincial force
PX—Post exchange
RAG—US Navy River Assault Group
RF—Regional force
R&R—Rest and recreation
TAOR—Tactical area of operations
TBS—The Basic School, Quantico, VA
TF—Task force
TQLC—Vietnamese Marine Corps
USNA—United States Naval Academy, Annapolis, MD
VC—Viet Cong
VNMC—Vietnamese Marine Corps
WIA—Wounded in action

US MILITARY OFFICER RANKS

ARMY, AIR FORCE	MARINE CORPS	NAVY
2nd Lieutenant	2nd Lt	Ensign
1st Lieutenant	1st Lt	Lieutenant Junior Grade
Captain	Capt	Lieutenant
Major	Maj	Lieutenant Commander
Lieutenant Colonel	LtCol	Commander
Colonel	Col	Captain
Brigadier General	BGen 1 star	Rear Admiral (lower half)
Major General	MGen 2 stars	Rear Admiral (upper half)
Lieutenant General	LtGen 3 stars	Vice Admiral
General	Gen 4 stars	Admiral

MAP OF SOUTH VIETNAM

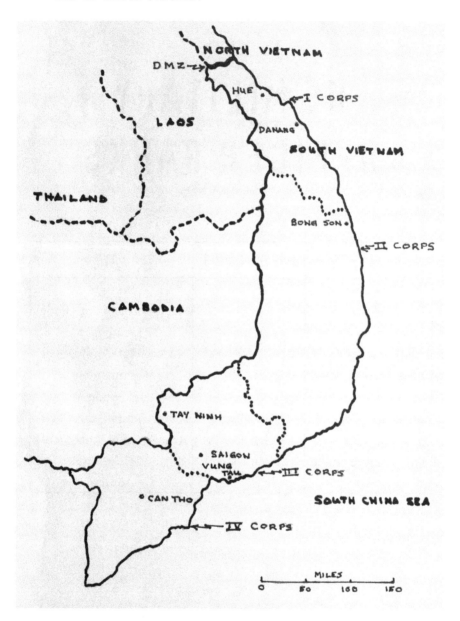

MAP OF HUÉ CITADEL

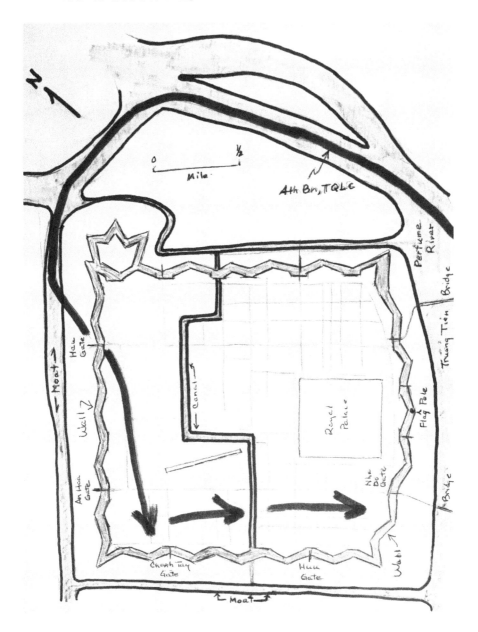